YEAR B
LENT/ EASTER

YEAR **B**

LENT/ EASTER

PREACHING

THE REVISED

COMMON

LECTIONARY

Marion Soards
Thomas Dozeman
Kendall McCabe

ABINGDON PRESS
Nashville

PREACHING THE REVISED COMMON LECTIONARY
YEAR B: LENT/EASTER

Copyright © 1993 by Abingdon Press

This book is printed on recycled, acid-free paper.

Library of Congress Cataloging-in-Publication Data
(Revised for vol. 2)

Soards, Marion L., 1952–
    Preaching the revised common lectionary.

    Contents: [1] Advent/Christmas/Epiphany—
[2] Lent/Easter.
    1. Bible—Homiletical use. 2. Lectionary preaching.
3. Advent. 4. Christmas. 5. Epiphany season.
I. Dozeman, Thomas B. II. McCabe, Kendall, 1939–
III. Common lectionary (1992). IV. Title.
BS534.5.S63   1993   251   92-36840
ISBN 0-687-33802-6 (v. 1)
ISBN 0-687-33803-4 (v. 2)

Scripture quotations, unless otherwise noted, are from the New Revised Standard
Version of the Bible, copyright 1989 by the Division of Christian Education of the
National Council of the Churches of Christ in the USA. Used by permission.

The responsive reading on pp. 46-47 is from the *Alternative Service Book 1980*.
Copyright © The Central Board of Finance of the Church of England.

93 94 95 96 97 98 99 00 01 — 10 9 8 7 6 5 4 3 2 1

MANUFACTURED IN THE UNITED STATES OF AMERICA

Contents

CONTENTS

This is one volume in a twelve-volume series. Each volume contains commentary and worship suggestions for a portion of lectionary cycle A, B, or C. Since the lectionary for a few special days do not change from one lectionary cycle to another, material for each of these days appears in only one of the volumes. Appropriate cross references in the table of contents lead the reader to material in other volumes of the series.

Introduction

Now pastors and students have a systematic treatment of essential issues of the Christian year and Bible study for worship and proclamation based on the Revised Common Lectionary. Interpretation of the lectionary will separate into three parts: Calendar, Canon, and Celebration. A brief word of introduction will provide helpful guidelines for utilizing this resource in worship through the Christian year.

Calendar. Every season of the Christian year will be introduced with a theological interpretation of its meaning, and how it relates to the overall Christian year. This section will also include specific liturgical suggestions for the season.

Canon. The lectionary passages will be interpreted in terms of their setting, structure, and significance. First, the word *setting* is being used loosely in this commentary to include a range of different contexts in which biblical texts can be interpreted from literary setting to historical or cultic settings. Second, regardless of how the text is approached under the heading of setting, interpretation will always proceed to an analysis of the structure of the text under study. Third, under the heading of significance, central themes and motifs of the passage will be underscored to provide a theological interpretation of the text as a springboard for preaching. Thus interpretation of the lectionary passages will result in the outline on the next page.

Celebration. This section will focus on specific ways of relating the lessons to liturgical acts and/or homiletical options for the day on which they occur. How the texts have been used in the Christian tradition will sometimes be illustrated to stimulate the thinking of preachers and planners of worship services.

I. OLD TESTAMENT TEXTS

A. The Old Testament Lesson

1. *Setting*
2. *Structure*
3. *Significance*

B. Psalm

1. *Setting*
2. *Structure*
3. *Significance*

II. NEW TESTAMENT TEXTS

A. The Epistle

1. *Setting*
2. *Structure*
3. *Significance*

B. The Gospel

1. *Setting*
2. *Structure*
3. *Significance*

Why We Use the Lectionary

Although many denominations have been officially or unofficially using some form of the lectionary for many years now, some pastors are still unclear about where it comes from, why some lectionaries differ from denomination to denomination, and why the use of a lectionary is to be preferred to a more random sampling of scripture.

Simply put, the use of a lectionary guarantees a more diverse scriptural diet for God's people when the bread of life is broken on the Lord's Day, and it can help protect the congregation from the whims and prejudices of the pastor and other worship planners. Faithful use of the lectionary means that preachers must deal with texts they had rather ignore, but about which the congregation may have great concern and interest. The Ascension narrative, which we encounter in this volume on the Seventh Sunday of Easter, might be a case in point. Adherence to the lectionary can be an antidote to that homiletical arrogance that says, "I know what my people need," and in humility acknowledges that the Word of God found in scripture may speak to more needs on Sunday morning than we even know exist, when we seek to proclaim faithfully the message we have wrestled from the text.

The lectionary may also serve as a resource for liturgical content. The psalm is intended to be a response to the Old Testament lesson in any case (and not read as a lesson itself), but beyond that, the lessons may inform the content of prayers of confession, intercession, and petition. Some lessons may be adapted as affirmations of faith, as in *The United Methodist Hymnal,* nos. 887-889. The "Celebration" entries for each day will call attention to these opportunities from time to time.

Pastors and preachers in the free church tradition should think of the lectionary as a primary resource for preaching and worship, but need to remember that the lectionary was made for them and not they for the lectionary. The lectionary may serve as the inspiration for a separate series of lessons and sermons that will include texts not in the present edition, or having chosen one of the lectionary passages as the basis for the day's sermon, the preacher may wish to make an independent choice of the other lessons in order to supplement and illustrate the primary text. The lectionary will be of most value when its use is not a cause for legalism but for inspiration.

As there are no perfect preachers, so there are no perfect lectionaries. The Revised Common Lectionary, upon which this series is based, is the result of the work of many years by the Consultation on Common Texts, and is a response to ongoing evaluation of the Common Lectionary (1983) by pastors and scholars from the several participating denominations. The current interest in the lectionary can be traced back to the Second Vatican Council, which ordered lectionary revision for the Roman Catholic Church:

> The treasures of the Bible are to be opened up more lavishly, so that richer fare may be provided for the faithful at the table of God's Word. In this way a more representative portion of the holy Scriptures will be read to the people over a set cycle of years. (Walter Abbott, ed., *The Documents of Vatican II* [Piscataway, N.J.: New Century, 1974], p. 155)

The example thus set by the Roman Catholics inspired the Protestants to take more seriously the place of the Bible in their services and sermons, and soon many denominations had issued their own three-year cycles, based generally on the Roman model but with their own modifications. This explains why some discrepancies and variations appear in different forms of the lectionary. The Revised Common Lectionary (RCL) is an effort to increase agreement among the churches. A table at the end of the volume will list the differences between the RCL and the Roman, Episcopal, and Lutheran lectionaries. Where no entry is made for the latter, their use accords with the RCL.

For those unacquainted with the general pattern of the lectionary, a brief word of explanation may be helpful. (1) The three years are each distinguished by one of the Synoptic Gospels: Matthew in A, Mark in B, Luke in C. John is distributed over the three years with a heavy emphasis during Lent and Easter. (2) Two types of readings are used. During the periods of Advent to Epiphany and Lent to Pentecost, the readings are usually topical—that is, there is some common theme among them. During the Sundays after Epiphany and after Pentecost the readings are continuous, with no necessary connection between the lessons. During the period from Ash Wednesday through the Day of Pentecost, there will usually be a thematic connection between the lessons. The preacher begins, then, with at least four preaching options: to deal with either one of the lessons on their own or to work with the theme shared by the lessons. Perhaps it should also be added that though the psalm is intended to be a response by the people to the Old Testament lesson, rather than being read as a lesson on its own, that in no way suggests that it cannot be used as the text for the sermon.

This is the second of four volumes that deal with the lessons for all of Year B of the Christian year. Volume 1 dealt with Advent through the time after Epiphany. Volume 3 begins with Trinity Sunday (the First Sunday After Pentecost) and includes all the lessons for June, July, and August. Volume 4 finishes the remainder of the year, including the lessons for All Saints' Day (November 1) and Thanksgiving Day. A new series will then be published for Year C.

A note on language: We have used the term *Old Testament* in this series because that is the language employed by the Consultation on Common Texts, at least up to this point. Pastors and worship committees may wish to consider alternative terms such as *First Testament* or *Hebrew Scriptures* that do not imply that those writings somehow have less value than the rest of the Christian Bible. Another option is to refer to *First Lesson* (always from the Hebrew Scriptures), *Second Lesson* (from Acts or the epistles), and *Gospel.*

THE MIND OF CHRIST IN LENT

Lent is probably the most widely observed season in the Christian year. Churches that ignore Advent, prefer Mother's Day to Pentecost, and isolate the observance of Christmas and Easter to one day each per year, are capable of mounting Lenten programs and special emphases on such a scale as to make the Easter sunrise service seem anticlimactic. Religion breaks out all over. The inoculation, in the form of regular church attendance for several weeks, usually works, however, for by the Sunday after Easter Day, few pietistic eruptions are to be seen remaining on the body ecclesiastical. Too bad that so much preparation often has so little payoff.

The purpose of this essay is not to provide a different program with a guaranteed long-range payoff, but rather to help those who plan worship and preach think about what they are doing in light of that entire period of time from Ash Wednesday to the Day of Pentecost and to see it as an unbroken chain of days that links us to and makes us one with the apostolic church and its experience of the saving Christ-event.

It is important to remember that Easter Day was originally the only day in the Christian year! The early Christians met weekly on the first day of the week to pray, to break bread, and to share in the apostles' reminiscences of Jesus' earthly ministry (Acts 2:42). Their meetings were characterized by an expectation of their Lord's immediate, sudden return. In this ecstatic atmosphere one did not do long-range planning and goal setting! But even within the pages of the New Testament we have indications that time is fast becoming a threat to Christian faith. Second Peter 3 is an effort to counter the arguments of the scoffers who deride the Christian hope. The answer that in the Lord's sight a thousand years are as one day might help relieve some of the Christian anxiety, but it did not change the fact that the Christians still had to make it through one day at a time on earthly calendars. Time, then, if it was not to be an enemy, had to be made a friend. It was through this domestication of time that the Christian year evolved.

The precise details of the evolution are impossible to know, varying as they doubtless did from region to region. The general outline is rather easy to discern. First there was the weekly celebration of the Resurrection. This celebration was of the entire Paschal mystery: the Incarnation, the Crucifixion, the Resurrection and Ascension, the gift of the Spirit, and the promise of the Lord's return. There next emerged a special emphasis in the spring on the celebration of the Paschal feast in relation to the actual time it had happened in history. This celebration extended itself back through the Crucifixion on Friday and the Last Supper on Thursday, thus creating the Paschal Triduum of Maundy Thursday, Good Friday, and Easter Eve (which carried over into Easter Day). We know that at Jerusalem the custom was begun of having the bishop ride a donkey into the city on the Sunday before the Passion and so inaugurate that period of observance that we call Holy Week. Just as the discrete events leading up to the Resurrection were separated for celebration, so two other events that had been seen as part of the whole Paschal mystery were also given individual recognition: the Ascension forty days after Easter Day and the anointing by the Holy Spirit at Pentecost fifty days after.

Lent emerged in the form in which we know it today as a combination of the church's catechetical program and penitential discipline. It was catechetical in that it was the final period of intense instruction before the catechumens were brought to the bishop to be baptized at Easter. This was seen as the most appropriate time for baptism, since through that action the catechumens fully put on Christ by dying and rising with him in the tomb of the font. One cannot emphasize too much the interrelationship of baptism and instruction here. *The Apostolic Tradition* of Hippolytus indicates that catechumens were to be instructed for three years, and that a catechumen who was slain for the faith prior to baptism "will be justified, for he has received baptism in his blood" (chap. 19). The rule seemed to be "no baptism without catechesis." Lent may be a good time to remind ourselves of this principle, not only as we continue the traditional Lenten confirmation classes, but as we also seek to establish classes for parents who will be bringing infants for baptism. The lessons for the Sundays in Lent in Year A are designed to be used in a nurturing process for catechumens or confirmands in preparation for Easter baptism and confirmation. In Years B and C, when other lessons are read on Sunday morning, the lessons of Year A may still be used for personal devotion or study in the confirmation class itself.

Penitential discipline came to be attached to Lent as the church came increasingly to understand itself as the field where the wheat and the weeds grew together. A major disagreement in the second century had to do with how to deal with those who denied or betrayed the faith during times of persecution. Those of a more rigorous disposition were in favor of excommunication and expulsion with no second chance allowed. The more catholic view prevailed, however, so that those who had sinned were expected to perform appropriate penance and during Lent were finally prepared to be received back fully into the fellowship of the church during Holy Week in time to be able to celebrate the Easter mysteries once more with the faithful. It soon became customary for all Christians to use the Lenten period as a time for repentance of past sins and self-denial (hence "giving things up" for Lent), even if their sins had not been of a major or notorious kind.

It is this history which is briefly described in many Ash Wednesday liturgies, such as the following from the *New Handbook of the Christian Year* (p. 112):

Dear brothers and sisters in Christ: Christians have always observed with great devotion the days of our Lord's passion and resurrection. It became the custom of the church to prepare for Easter by a season of penitence, fasting, and prayer. This season of forty days provided a time in which converts to the faith were prepared for baptism into the body of Christ. It is also the time when persons who had committed serious sins and had been separated from the community of faith were reconciled by penitence and forgiveness, and restored to the fellowship of the church. The whole congregation is thus reminded of the mercy and forgiveness proclaimed in the gospel of Jesus Christ and the need we all have to renew our baptismal faith.

Preachers and planners of worship ought then to keep in mind these two primary purposes of the Lenten season: the training of candidates for baptism and confirmation and the encouragement of the whole congregation to renewed dedication and commitment.

Lent is not a prolonged meditation upon the Passion and death of Christ, a pre-extended Good Friday. The clue to the meaning of Lent can be found by looking at the two days that bracket it, Ash Wednesday and Good Friday. On Ash Wednesday it is customary in many congregations for persons to have ashes placed upon their heads while they are being told, "Remember that you are dust, and to dust you shall return." In other words, we are confronted by the fact of our mortality in a vivid physical encounter. On Good Friday we witness the death of another human being, and we are told that in that death we all have died. Lent certainly is intended to end at the cross, but its emphasis in Year B is to remind us of the series of covenants into which God has entered with humanity and which reaches a climax in the baptismal covenant of the Paschal liturgy for which Lent is the time of preparation. The First Sunday in Lent begins with God's promise to Noah, the covenant between "God and every living creature of all flesh that is on the earth." Already we are being reminded that the water which was a judgment unto death for sin will become for us a sign of God's saving power.

The lessons through Lent provide an opportunity to examine ourselves in relation to the mystery of the cross as a sign of the new covenant and to examine ourselves in terms of the covenant we made with God through baptism or which we expect to make if we are preparing for baptism or confirmation. As we did not celebrate Advent pretending Christmas had not happened, so we do not celebrate Lent as though we know nothing about Easter. Lent is a time of "festive fasting," in the words of Adrian Nocent:

> In the early Christian centuries the faithful thought that [Christ's] return would take place during the night between Holy Saturday and Easter Sunday, since that night was the center of Christian life, being the anniversary of Christ's victory and the moment when that victory became present anew. The fast that marked the Vigil, and indeed the whole Lenten fast, is festive because it is leading up to the victory and return of the Spouse. [*The Liturgical Year 2: Lent,* p. 41]

The traditional color in the West for Lent has been purple, recognizing that we are decorating for the king who is on his way to mount the throne of the cross. The medieval English use of the "Lenten array" has been increasingly adopted by many churches.

This involves the use of unbleached linen for the paraments. Any decorative symbols such as crosses are not embroidered on, but are painted, usually in black, red, cream, or some combination of those three. The altar or communion table would be completely covered all around, giving it a coffin-like appearance. Brass or metal altarware would be replaced by a simple cross and candlesticks of wood, or else the cross would be entirely draped in the same kind of unbleached material and tied at the base. The lack of any altar flowers is also appropriate during Lent in preparation for the floral explosion that usually marks the Easter proclamation.

The lessons for Ash Wednesday do not change during the three-year cycle. Since they were discussed in the Year A series (Lent/Easter), the reader is referred there for commentary. Also, because of space limitations, the Easter Vigil service commentary is to be found in Lent/Easter of the Year A series, and the Holy or Maundy Thursday commentary will appear in Lent/Easter of the Year C series.

First Sunday in Lent

Old Testament Texts

Genesis 9:8-17 is the story of God's covenant with Noah at the close of the flood and Psalm 25:1-10 is a prayer song of petitions and expressions of trust.

The Lesson: *Genesis 9:8-17*

God's Obligation to Remember

Setting. Genesis 9:8-17 must be read in the larger context of the flood in Genesis 6–9. The flood is God's first attempt to eradicate evil from the world, and, as such, it is a failure. No amount of water is able to purify the curse (3:17) that God had earlier let loose on the earth because of the sin of humans. Genesis 6–9 contains two interpretations of just how much of a failure the flood in fact was. In the Yahwistic account the flood is a complete failure. It is prompted when God envisions the wickedness of humans as being so complete that they could not even imagine good things (6:5-8), and this situation is unchanged in the end (8:20-22). Note the repetition in these two texts concerning the evil inclination of the human heart. This repetition underscores that the stain in the human heart has not been bleached out by the flood waters, and, in view of this, it is as though God decides not to wear out the rest of the garment of creation by working on the stain.

The lesson for this Sunday is from the priestly conclusion to the flood story (9:1-17). The flood is not a divine success story in the priestly version any more than it was in the Yahwistic account. It is not, however, the utter failure of the earlier version, and the reason for this is the change of focus in the conclusion from human sin to God. If the flood is read from the point of view of humans (the Yahwistic account), it is a pointless tragedy since the dark heart of humanity remains unchanged. If the flood is read with an eye on God (the priestly account), it becomes a more meaningful story since this tragedy does change God. The lesson for this Sunday probes the changes in God after the flood, by introducing the motif of covenant.

Structure. Genesis 9:8-17 is the second half of the priestly conclusion to the flood. Genesis 9:1-17 separates into two parts. Verses 1-7 focus on humans at the close of the flood. These verses are not any more positive than the Yahwistic ending to the flood. Even though God blesses Noah, humanity is not pictured in a positive manner. Humans exit the ark as carnivorous meat eaters instead of vegetarians, and God makes concessions for this fact by introducing prohibitions about drinking blood and about killing other humans. The end result of this situation is that humans project an aura of terror and dread over the rest of creation (v. 2). Verses 8-17 shift the focus from humans to God. Note how v. 9 begins with the divine speech, "As for me. . . ." Verses 8-17 separate into two parts: vv. 8-11 introduce the motif of covenant, and vv. 12-17 describe how the rainbow is a sign of the covenant.

Significance. How does God change at the end of the flood? This question must be answered by examining the two parts of vv. 8-17. The introduction of covenant in vv. 8-11 provides the primary clue of how God changes. Thus it requires definition. There is debate over what it means to be in covenant. Does it signify a relationship between two parties or simply the obligations that must be fulfilled in contracts. Covenant is used at a number of points in the Old Testament to describe mutual agreements between persons. For example, Abraham and Abimelech (Genesis 21:27), Isaac and Abimelech (Genesis 26:28), and Jacob and Laban (Genesis 31:44) all make covenants with each other for different reasons. In each of these cases both individuals are willing and equal partners in a contract, which forms a relationship. In these situations both meanings of covenant appear to be present (obligation and relationship). Covenant in Genesis 9:8-11, however, does not fit the pattern of the previous examples because the parties are not equal in the story. Thus, even though upon first reading the language does appear to be relational—between God and Noah (vv. 12, 15), all living creatures (vv. 12, 15, 16), and the earth (v. 13)—no agreements are made that require a response from Noah or anything else in creation. In fact, Noah does not even speak in the narrative. At most he provides a backdrop for a series of declarations by God about covenant, which function as a divine self-description. Genesis 9:8-17, therefore, must be viewed as God's story, and covenant must be interpreted as providing insight into obligations that God takes on after the flood.

What are these obligations and how do they signal change in the character of God? First, the content of covenant provides the clue of what changes occur in God's character. God rejects his previous commitment to destroy, and seals the rejection legally with a covenant. Second, by sealing his decision not to destroy in a covenant without conditions, we learn that God is not free. Note how Genesis 9:11 reads, "never again" will there be a flood. Third, by giving up the freedom to destroy, God is making a commitment to this world, which creates a future hope.

The significance of the flood for the priestly writer is that God can no longer abandon this world, but is obligated to work with it. The rainbow in vv. 12-17 is a sign that forces God to remember this obligation. What may be viewed as bad for God is certainly good for humans, for it means that the inability of humans to imagine good things can no longer be the final word as it was for the Yahwistic account of the flood. Instead hope is the final word. Hope, however, as the sign of the rainbow makes clear, does not lie with Noah or Noah's relationship with God, but in God's commitment to covenant and in God's ability to remember this commitment (v. 16). Thus the rainbow takes on an important function in the context of covenant, for it is meant to remind God of a change in character from being one who freely destroys to becoming a God who manifests unending obligation to this world. This is certainly the point of focus for preaching this text, and it gives rise to a second point—namely, that our hope lies in God, rather than in any perceived changes in ourselves.

The Response: *Psalm 25:1-10*

A Petition for God to Remember

Setting. Psalm 25:1-10 is acrostic (each line begins with a letter of the Hebrew alphabet). Thus the form is somewhat rigid, which has prompted debate concerning whether it is a lament or a petitionary prayer. Three aspects of this psalm provide important background for interpretation, which also ties back to Genesis 9:8-17. One, the petitioner is surrounded by enemies (v. 2). Two, the petitioner is not without guilt in whatever the situation may be (v. 8). In other words, Psalm 25 is not about the suffering of the innocent. And, third, in this ambiguous situation of "enemies" and a "guilty" person, the focus is starkly on God and God's character. Hope does not lie in either the enemies or the petitioner, but in God's character—more precisely in God's ability to remember (vv. 6-7). The focus on God for hope is very similar to the priestly ending of the flood story.

Structure. Psalm 25:1-10 separates into two parts. In vv. 1-7 the petitioner expresses trust in God while presenting a series of requests. In vv. 8-10 the focus shifts from the situation of the psalmist to the character of God. These verses present a series of divine attributes that provide the basis for the trust expressed in v. 1.

Significance. Verses 1-2 anchor the focus of the psalm in God, "To you, O LORD, I lift up my soul. O my God, in you I trust." These verses key us in to the fact that the psalm is not introspection. The focus is on God and what God is able to do, and it is this divine activity that provides the basis for trust. The petitions move in three directions in vv. 1-7. One is about the enemies (vv. 2-3)—that they not be allowed to overtake the psalmist. The second petition focuses on the psalmist and her relationship with God (vv. 4-6)—that God teach her divine truth. The third petition provides an interesting connection to Genesis 9:8-17, for it is an appeal for divine memory. God is called upon in vv. 6-7 to remember the ancient divine quality of steadfast love (v. 6), which can erase the recent transgression of the psalmist (v. 7). Hope, here, does not lie in any change within the psalmist, but in the character of God, which is also the situation at the close of the flood. Petitions give way to affirmations about the character of God in vv. 8-10, which repeat much of the language in vv. 4-7.

New Testament Texts

Both New Testament lessons include references to baptism and suffering or temptation, and in both passages Jesus Christ is a model and a present and real help to believers. I Peter 3:18-22 explores how baptism allows Christians to live in the Spirit of Jesus even in times of suffering. Mark's account informs us that even Christ himself was tempted after being baptized, and we learn not only that he was able to withstand temptation but also that his move to faithful fulfillment of the ministry for which he came forth occurred only after he passed through the time of his trials.

The Epistle: *I Peter 3:18-22*

Being Saved Through Baptism

Setting. The larger section in which our lesson occurs is I Peter 3:13-22. In this larger passage the author encourages his audience to endure unjust suffering and, then, he offers Jesus as an example. The situation of the present believers and the past action of Jesus is brought together at the end of the passage through a discussion of baptism. In so doing baptism is presented as a link between Jesus and the present believers, which provides the power for Christians to endure even unjust suffering. The meaning of baptism will be our focus in examining the lesson.

Structure. I Peter 3:18-22 focuses on the suffering and death of Jesus in order to provide a theological framework for believers to endure wrongful affliction in the present time. The passage is quite deliberately constructed and can be outlined in the following way:

The Reasons Why There Can Be Blessing Even in Suffering (3:18-22)
   A. Jesus died in the flesh (3:18*a*)
   B. Jesus lives in the Spirit (3:18*b*)
   C. The meaning of baptism in the light of the journey of Jesus through hell and into heaven (3:19-22)
      1. Noah (and the others) were saved through the flood
      2. Christians are saved through baptism

Baptism here is the sign, symbol, and seal of God's covenant through Jesus Christ who has already expressed the saving grace of God in his death, Resurrection, and exaltation. As Jesus Christ died and lives, because Jesus Christ died and lives, Christians are able to endure and triumph over the suffering they experience in the course of their lives.

Significance. The lesson outlines, first, what our hope is by remembering the Passion of Jesus, and, second, reflects upon how we know the will of God in the present time through baptism. The meditation on the Passion of Jesus has three parts: (1) Jesus died in the flesh as the result of unjust suffering (3:18*a*), (2) he lives in the Spirit (3:18*b*), and (3) he has even journeyed through hell and into heaven (3:19-22). Jesus' life in the Spirit introduces a comparison between the past saving of Noah (and seven others) and the present salvation of Christians. In this vein the author explores the meaning of baptism. What is the nature of the analogy? The affinity between the experience of Noah and the Christian is not simply a similarity between the water of the flood and the water of baptism. Rather the analogy drawn here is between the salvation of Noah and his family through water and the salvation of Christians through baptism. The analogy underscores how baptism is not a psychological rite of passage, but quite literally the movement from one world to another—as the ark carried Noah's family through the flood to another world so the believer moves from the sin-fraught context of the current world into the new creation brought by God's work in Jesus Christ. Entering this new world through baptism alters the believer, for it applies the benefits of Christ's death and resurrection to us, which results in spiritual transformation. In other words, we see the world differently in baptism—with a clear conscience or to use a biblical metaphor, we regard the world with a transformed mind—because we have, in fact, entered a different world of which the church is the first emerging sign. It is only when we have two feet firmly planted in this new world (the kingdom ushered in by Jesus which is being manifested in his church) that we know what our hope is, what proper fear of God entails (and why we need not fear any other power), and, finally, what constitutes unjust suffering. The crucial message inherent in I Peter is that only the church as a collective body can decide what is unjust suffering. As individuals we cannot make this discernment. Our baptism makes this point clear, for it is a collective sacrament, a celebration of the covenant, which grafts each of us into the body of the Christ.

Finally, baptism is not magic. It is a celebration of covenant faith—and, both the covenant and the faith are gifts from God. We participate in salvation; it radically affects us, but it is not our achievement. It is the work of God (Christ has died, Christ has been raised, Christ is exalted at the right hand of God, and all power and authority is his!) that accomplishes our salvation.

The Gospel: *Mark 1:9-15*

The Journey of Faith: From Baptism Through Temptation to Faithfulness

Setting. After the opening of the Gospel (v. 1) and the report of the appearance and ministry of John the Baptist (vv. 2-8), Mark brings Jesus himself onto the scene. He is baptized (vv. 9-11), he is tempted (vv. 12-13), and then he comes forth preaching (vv. 14-15). The story begun in vv. 14-15 continues through the Gospel running up to and perhaps through the Passion Narrative in chapters 14–16.

Structure. Mark 1:1-11 is called the prologue to the story of Jesus' ministry. Our lesson includes the final three verses of Mark's introductory materials, recalling the baptism of Jesus. (Readers may wish to consult the comments on the Gospel lesson for the First Sunday After the Epiphany, Year B, for additional information on vv. 9-11.) Following this introductory section, vv. 12-13 recall an interlude between the time of the ministry of John the Baptist and the beginning of Jesus' own public work. In turn, vv. 14-15 recall the launching of Jesus' ministry and begins to tell of Jesus' words and deeds. (Readers may wish to consult the comments on the Gospel lesson for the Third Sunday After the Epiphany, Year B, for additional information on vv. 14-15.)

Significance. Notice the sequence of Jesus' experiences comprised by the verses of our lesson: from baptism through temptation to ministry. From this order of events we see that our Lord Jesus Christ stands in actual, not merely ideological or emotional, solidarity with his followers. From the powerful beginning of baptism, which means that Jesus was anointed with the Spirit, he moves to doing ministry only after and through being tempted.

The immediate temptation we face in reading this lesson is to ask,

How could Christ be tempted? or, Why was Christ tempted? But, while Matthew and Luke show more interest in giving details about Jesus' being tempted in their editions of the gospel (see Matthew 4:1-11 and Luke 4:1-13), Mark's brief account merely provides sufficient information and imagery to show that the temptation of Jesus was part of the cosmic conflict between the heavenly forces of good and the hellish forces of evil. The setting in the wilderness and the mention of wild beasts would tip any first-century person to the demonic setting in which Jesus is tempted. The wilderness was considered to be a habitat of demons and wild beasts were associated with them, often as animals that were demon possessed. Moreover, the story states bluntly that Satan tempted Jesus and that angels ministered to him. Notice that Mark does not say that Jesus was tempted for forty days by Satan and, then, angels appeared to minister to him. Matthew gives us that sequence, in part because he focuses during the forty days on the exchanges between Jesus and the devil. Mark's story seems to assume, however, that throughout the time of temptation Jesus was the one wooed by Satan and attended to by God's angels. In the power of the Spirit our Lord faced temptation, and through the gracious help of God he emerges from the trials victorious and prepared for his public ministry.

Mark's account tells us many things, but for proclamation two items stand out. First, being baptized and having the presence and power of the Holy Spirit granted to us is no insulation against real struggles with the forces of evil. Christian faith (or, commitment and spirituality) is not an exemption from temptation. Rather, baptism and God's grace are preparation and provision for the real encounters with evil that we experience in this world. Second, while temptation (in any one of many forms from enticement to suffering) is neither God's direct activity nor the result of God's actions, God is with us in our moments of trial. Indeed, God may even use the very real perils of satanic temptation to strengthen, refine, prepare, motivate, and direct us into accomplishing his will. The promise of faith is that one day God will wipe away all tears, but in the present age where death and destruction are still with us, God's grace grows roses from ashes by defying evil in the process of ultimately defeating it.

The message of costly grace, which comes as good news to

Christians, is that in Jesus Christ we have a Lord who fully sympathizes with us, both in our moments of exaltation and temptation. The promise of his presence in our lives is the guarantee from God that we will not be overcome by evil. Rather, under the lordship of Jesus Christ we are called to walk securely through life's trials to live faithfully and freely in relation to God's will.

Lent 1: The Celebration

In his lectures on Genesis, Martin Luther concludes his remarks on the story of Noah by entering into a long excursus on the function of allegory in biblical interpretation with particular attention to the flood narrative. Although he is generally opposed to allegory, he maintains that there are some examples ''which are made to agree with the analogy of the faith,'' and of these he approves. On his approved list is I Peter 3:21-22, part of the epistle reading for today. About that he says:

> Peter declares that we, too, are saved through water in Baptism, which is symbolized by the Flood, because pouring water over us or immersing us is death. And yet from that death or immersion there arises life because of the ark in which we are preserved, that is, because of the Word of promise to which we hold fast. The canonical Scriptures put forth this allegory, and it is something not only trustworthy but also worthwhile in every way. We should consider it carefully, for it provides glorious comfort even in extreme perils. (*Luther's Works*, vol. 2, Jaroslav Pelikan, ed. [St. Louis: Concordia, 1960], p. 155)

It should be noted that Luther does not identify the ark with the church, as in the World Council of Church's logo, but with the Word of God in which we can trust. His emphasis is particularly appropriate today when the focus of the Old Testament lesson is on the rainbow and God's word of promise.

John Calvin saw an analogy with ''word of promise/rainbow'' and ''word/sacrament.'' This may lead the preacher to a discussion of the two Paschal sacraments for which Lent is the time of preparation and of how the sacramental elements receive their meaning in relation to what God has said and done in the mystery of redemption. The sacraments may also be used to illustrate God's faithful presence in the midst of a tempted life, of a tempted congregation. What is important about the rainbow is that God will remember. Just as there is no implied threat here that if humanity forgets the meaning of the rainbow the thunder will start to roll, so our cognitive apprehension of God in the sacraments is not required for our reception of those "inestimable benefits."

George Matheson's hymn, "O Love That Wilt Not Let Me Go," with its reference to "the rainbow through the rain," also picks up other themes from today's lessons.

The epistle lesson provides the scriptural basis for the line in the Apostles' Creed that refers to Jesus' descent among the dead. And, since the Apostles' Creed is the traditional baptismal creed of the Church, its use would be particularly fitting today.

The reference to eight people in the epistle suggests how significant the number eight is in baptismal imagery. Easter, the day of baptism, is the eighth day of creation, the day of the new creation, as is Pentecost when the Church was born in a baptism of fire. The preacher may wish to see if the font in the church has eight sides (most of them do).

Second Sunday in Lent

Old Testament Texts

Genesis 17:1-7, 15-16 is the account of the initiation of circumcision, while Psalm 22:23-31 provides language for the offspring of Jacob who learn how to praise when God answers during times of testing.

The Lesson: *Genesis 17:1-7, 15-16*

The Nature of Divine Promises

Setting. Genesis 17 is the priestly account of God making a covenant with Abraham. This chapter occurs in a larger section of stories that center around the problems of Abraham and Sarah in having a child. The tension created by the problem of infertility is theological, since God promised Abraham in Genesis 12:1-4 that he and Sarah would have many children.

Structure. Genesis 17 separates into two parts that mirror each other. Genesis 17:1-14 consists of a divine theophany to Abraham, which separates into four parts. It begins in vv. 1-2 with a divine revelation of the name "God Almighty" and the promise of covenant. Verse 3 is a response of worship by Abraham. Verses 4-8 provide content to the divine promise of covenant through a series of promises: Abraham will be fruitful, nations and kings will be his offspring, he will receive the land of his sojourning as his own possession, and these promises are unconditional. The effect of these promises on Abraham is that he goes through a name change (from Abram to Abraham). Verses 9-14 are a divine speech that outlines what Abraham must do in this covenant relationship, which is to circumcise all the males in his household.

Genesis 17:15-27 repeats the cycle of the first half of the chapter, only this time the focus is on Sarah. Abraham receives a promise in vv. 15-16 that Sarah will have a child. The effect of this promise is a name change (from Sarai to Sarah). Verse 17 is a response by Abraham. Again he worships, but he also laughs at the idea of Sarah being pregnant. Verses 18-22 are more detailed promises concerning Isaac and Ishmael. Then the chapter ends in vv. 23-27 with an account of Abraham performing circumcision.

Significance. The outline of Genesis 17 underscores how the lectionary text includes only the opening promises to Abraham (vv. 1-7) and Sarah (vv. 15-16). These narrow boundaries invite reflection on the nature of divine promise. Especially how the divine promises to Abraham are unconditional, that is not dependent on any particular response by Abraham. If the theme of promise is pursued as the topic of a sermon, then at the very least the lectionary text should be expanded to include v. 8, since it functions at the apex of divine promise in this chapter. The tension between the present infertility of Sarah and the promise of a child is paralleled by Abraham's status as a sojourner and God's promise of land. This tension gives the text an eschatological perspective that provides the context for probing the meaning of faith.

The Response: *Psalm 22:23-31*

A Thanksgiving

Setting. Psalm 22 separates into two very different parts. Verses 1-21 are a lament in which the psalmist petitions God for salvation from a great distance. The focus changes to thanksgiving in vv. 22-31 in light of God's response. Psalm 22, therefore, covers the vast range of language in the psalter from dispair to joy. The lectionary text picks up the language of thanksgiving in the second half of the psalm.

Structure. It is difficult to break vv. 23-31 into smaller structures. It is worth noting, however, that the second half of the psalm actually begins in v. 22, when the psalmist addresses the congregation in worship with the intent to praise God. The setting of praise, therefore, is firmly anchored in the worshiping community, which is identified as the offspring of the ancestors.

Significance. The distress of the psalmist in vv. 1-21 provides a prelude for the thanksgiving in the second half of the psalm. Two things in vv. 23-31 stand out when it is read in conjunction with Genesis 17. The first is the setting of worship that is underscored in vv. 22 and 25. The second is the emphasis on the people of God as being those who ''fear the Lord.'' The psalm reinforces how the fear of God is an essential character of the people of God.

New Testament Texts

In quite different ways the lessons pose a truly basic question, What or whom do you trust in attempting to live a Christian life? Paul points away from the law to faith as the way in which we are related to God, and Jesus calls Peter away from Satan and self to follow him (Jesus). Faith as foundation, God as saving power, Jesus Christ as master, and obedience as the way of life for believers are the major motifs of these passages.

The Epistle: *Romans 4:13-25*

The Meaning of Faith

Setting. The entire fourth chapter of Romans is a reflection on Abraham—his person, his story, and his faith. Paul's discussion falls into clear parts. Verses 1-17 ponder three symbolic dimensions of the figure of Abraham in order to define the standard of God's work in justification. Then, in vv. 18-22 Paul presents Abraham as the exemplar of the human dimensions of faith. Finally, in 4:23-25 Paul personalizes his discourse by articulating the meaning of the Abraham story for himself and other believers.

Structure. The first segment of our lesson (vv. 13-17) states that Abraham received a promise from God and the promise was given to faith, not to the law. The second portion of the passage (vv. 18-22) makes it clear that faith is an unwavering confidence in God, not merely an intellectual act or the affirmation of a proposition. It is a hope against hope, because it is hope in God, not self. The third part of the lesson (vv. 23-35) relates Paul's thinking to the life of the believers: Abraham's God raised "Jesus our Lord from the dead" and now grants the same justification that was given to Abraham to all who believe in this God.

Significance. By taking up the figure of Abraham, Paul labors to establish and define the continuity of the gospel he preaches with the events and the testimony of the Old Testament. The entirety of Romans 4 is an appeal to scriptural precedence in order to establish the authenticity of Paul's proclamation. Paul's contention that God's righteousness is manifested independently of the law seems to fly in the face of the message of the Old Testament, so Paul demonstrates the correctness of his gospel by reaching back to the beginning of the story of Israel, to the very first Jew, the venerable Abraham. Paul retells portions of the story of God's dealings with Abraham to show that his message about the saving work of God in Jesus Christ is not an aberration, rather saving grace that grasps the lives of believers through faith is the outcome of God's plan, which was put in motion with Abraham. Paul understands that his appeal to this Old Testament story is an appeal to God himself, for Paul assumes with other first-century Jews and Christians that Scripture gives reliable access to God's actual truth, which is part of God's very self. (This is not to equate the Bible and God, but to claim that as the Bible speaks of God, God's own word is heard in the words of the Bible.)

Abraham received God's promise for the future. Thus, he is a prototype for Christians who recognize the fulfillment of that promise in Jesus Christ and, in turn, themselves receive the gift of justification and the promise of resurrection through faith in what God has done, is doing, and will do through Jesus Christ. Scholars debate whether "justification by grace through faith" is the center per se or a central portion of Paul's theology. Whichever is correct, notice that all giving attention to this matter agree that the basic idea, "justification by grace through faith," is a distinctive, crucial element of Paul's understanding and explanation of God's saving work through Christ. Paul declares this is who God is, and this is how God has related to humanity (at least) since the time of Abraham.

When we view the totality of God's plan from Abraham to Christ, we find that we become heirs to Abraham's legacy through the dynamics of promise and fulfillment rather than through the restrictive operation of the law. Looking from Abraham to Christ shows us that God is the God who justifies the ungodly. God is the one who created life and is the one who gives life to the dead. God, who is the Creator, acts to restore order to his creation, which has fallen into disarray, and now God promises to grant eternal life to believers as he raised Jesus Christ from the grave. In all of this, from start to finish, grace is God's method, faith is God's means, and righteousness is God's end. The "good news" is this: "What God promised, he has the power to do."

The Gospel: *Mark 8:31-38*

The Demand to Be Faithful

Setting. The following discussion of setting largely repeats information given in relation to the Gospel lesson for the Last Sunday After the Epiphany. The middle portion of Mark's Gospel, from 8:22 through 10:52, contains some of the most dramatic words and events of Jesus' ministry. The section opens and closes with different stories about Jesus' healing of blind men. Commentators often describe these healings as paradigms of the faith experience of the disciples who move through the Gospel from blindness to half-sight to seeing all things clearly; then, after they have thrown off the mantle of their ignorance through a full encounter with the Lord, they are able to follow him in the way which is his. Whether this helpful, but essentially allegorical, interpretation of the boundary-stories of the middle portion of Mark is correct, it is certainly the case that Mark 8:22–10:52 contains important information about the identity of Christ and true discipleship to him. Between the two stories about blind men, there are three recognizable and repetitive cycles of material: 8:31–9:30; 9:31–10:32; 10:33-45. Though the symmetry is not perfectly patterned, in each of these sections we find (1) a Passion prediction, (2) an ensuing misunderstanding on the part of the disciples, and (3) instruction(s) by Jesus on discipleship.

Structure. Our lesson is made up of the first Passion prediction by

Jesus and of the first instance of subsequent misunderstanding on the part of the disciples. The text as a whole presents a sharp exchange in conversation: Jesus teaches; Peter attempts to rebuke him; and Jesus incontrovertibly rebukes Peter, thus ending the dialogue and having the final say. Themes such as "Jesus' words are hard to hear" (paying careful attention to the particular words he utters here), and "sometimes we think we know better than the Lord" (picking up the pattern of misunderstanding here and at other places throughout Mark to build analogies to our misguided notions about relating to God today), and "Jesus corrects flawed faith to bring us into line" (some work with exegetically oriented commentaries will help) are appropriate topics for preaching—in concert or solo. Two seemingly common but wrong-headed approaches to this text either reduce Jesus to a model of "tough love" or suggest that Peter was in peril of being absolutely rejected as a disciple.

Significance. Jesus' foretelling of his suffering and death provokes and brings out the lack of comprehension of his disciples, in this instance Peter. How hard it is to hear about the necessity of the suffering of Christ. If Christ is the Lord, if Christ is indeed the Son of God, then Christ should be all powerful, regal, majestic, and sublime. The Lord should be above the fray of life in this world, and surely he should be beyond the nasty business of suffering. Yet in this lesson we hear him foretelling his Passion. Not only is he subject to the terrible forces that afflict us during life in this world, he knowingly anticipates the brutal reality of tribulation and declares his commitment to experience its devastating pain. And so, we understand Peter who, shocked at what he hears, upbraids Jesus for his teaching.

The verb used here, "to rebuke," is striking. It occurs twice in this passage: first, to state what Peter does to Jesus, and then, to describe what Jesus does to Peter. Elsewhere in Mark the verb is used to say what Jesus does to the demons he reproaches in exorcism. A strong word in Mark's vocabulary, "to rebuke" is to confront and to condemn with the purpose of effecting radical change. Peter hears Jesus. Only lines earlier in the story we heard Peter confess that Jesus was the Christ. Apparently Peter had a definition of the Messiah that was different from Jesus' own understanding. Peter's assumptions about the Christ were most likely colored by his time and culture; thus, he thought of the Christ as the promised heir of David or a similar figure of power. In other words, he wanted a Christ who would be a Jewish Caesar. Such a Christ would call disciples to position, privilege, power, and prestige—to a place past perfidious perils. Yet what does Peter find but Jesus talking about suffering and dying? Therefore, he does the only reasonable thing, he tries to set Jesus straight.

Jesus will have none of it! He comes back at Peter with the same intensity that Peter had aimed at him. Mark recounts the sharp retort (literally), "Get behind me, Satan! For you are not thinking the things of God but the things of humans." These are strange but terribly important words that are loaded with meaning. Two points demand attention: First, the command, "get behind me," employs some of the exact words ("behind me") with which Jesus initially called Peter to discipleship (see 1:17). Jesus does not say, "Get lost!" Rather, he demands that Peter step back into the place where Jesus called him to be—namely, into discipleship. Second, that Jesus seems rude in calling Peter "Satan" is far less disturbing than the correlation between Satan and "thinking the things of humans." Can it be that a purely human ambition, conjured up independently of God's will and set up with the best of intentions—even "for" God, but with human expectations—in the place of God's purposes, is sheerly satanic? The rebuke warns us that whenever we formulate plans for God, we are playing God and not being faithful. Disciples are called to follow, not to take over the lead.

Lent 2: The Celebration

The Old Testament text, psalm, and epistle for today draw attention to the progeny of faith. Abraham will become the ancestor of a multitude of nations; God's deliverance will be proclaimed to a people yet unborn; Paul recalls the promise made to Abraham in today's Old Testament lesson. The sermon may provide an opportunity to help those preparing for Easter baptism and confirmation to see themselves as part of the fulfillment of the promise. There are echoes here of the assertion in Hebrews 11:40 that even the giants of the faith will not

35

come to perfection until all God's children are gathered home. We stand as beneficiaries of the faith of those who have gone before us, and we have an obligation of faith to those who follow us. These texts are offered as an antidote to a religion that is so intensely personal and "faith centered" that it has no place for the communion of saints across time or that fails to see how the biblical witness is to the calling of "a people" rather than a conglomeration of individuals.

The following lines adapted from the psalm are suitable for a responsive call to worship:

> From God comes my praise in the great congregation;
> **my vows I will pay before those who fear God.**
> The poor shall eat and be satisfied;
> **and all the nations shall bow before God.**

The last versicle and response are particularly appropriate if the Lord's Supper is observed. The Old Testament lesson suggests "The God of Abraham Praise" as an opening hymn, and the epistle lesson "O For a Faith That Will Not Shrink" as its response or a sermon hymn, if faith is to be the subject for the day.

The epistle reading should provide the hermeneutical key to both the Old Testament and the Gospel readings. Abraham and Peter are contrasted by their faith response to God's call. If the Gospel reading is the primary text for the sermon, the preacher will need to be careful not to turn the exhortation to take up the cross into an exercise in works righteousness. Christian obedience is always a faith-full activity that demonstrates a radical trust and hope in a God who brings new life from a hundred-year-old body and from a tomb in Palestine.

" 'Take Up Thy Cross,' the Savior Said" is based upon the Gospel reading. A once popular hymn based on Mark 8:38, "Jesus, and Shall It Ever Be," is now found in few hymnals, although four stanzas have been printed in the *AMEC Bicentennial Hymnal* (no. 288). The following stanza is suggested as a response to the reading:

> Ashamed of Jesus! sooner far
> let evening blush to own a star;
> he sheds the beams of light divine
> o'er this benighted soul of mine.

Third Sunday in Lent

Old Testament Texts

Exodus 20:1-20 is the account of the revelation of divine law to Israel that occurred at Mount Sinai. Psalm 19 is a hymn that praises law.

The Lesson: *Exodus 20:1-17*

The Gift of Law

Setting. The most prominent event in Israel's wilderness journey is the revelation of law at Mount Sinai. After Israel is led out of Egypt in Exodus 15 their initial wilderness journey is described for 3 chapters (Exodus 16–18). In Exodus 19:1 the journey stops and the reader is informed that Israel arrived at Mount Sinai, where they prepare to meet God. The revelation of God to Israel at Mount Sinai continues for the next 72 chapters (Exodus 19–Numbers 10). In these chapters the Israelites do not journey, and, instead, they sit at the base of the mountain to receive revelation through laws that are meant to direct their worship and their communal life. When the story of Israel's journey to Canaan is resumed in Numbers 10, it only lasts for the remainder of this book, because the wilderness journey gives way again in Deuteronomy to the recounting of the gift of law, but this time the mountain is named Horeb instead of Sinai. This quick overview underscores how central law is in the larger story of Israel's salvation from Egypt, and how law defines Israel during the faith journey through the wilderness.

Exodus 20:1-17 contains the account of the revelation of the Decalogue, which is the first of many legal codes that will be revealed at Mount Sinai. A detailed interpretation of each of the Ten Commandments is not possible in the limited space of the present commentary, and the reader is advised to use a current commentary on Exodus to achieve this goal. The aim of this commentary will be more general—namely, to interpret the central role of law as a divine gift of salvation to Israel. Such a goal is important because frequently Christians are robbed of this gift because they view the law as a burden that was discarded after Christ.

Structure. Exodus 20:1-17 must be read in the larger context of theophany in Exodus 19. The first part of Exodus 19 narrates Israel's arrival at Mount Sinai and their preparation for theophany. In vv. 10-15 Moses is given specific instructions on how Israel was to purify (and thus protect) themselves for the descent of God in fire that is described in vv. 16-19. The giving of the Decalogue in Exodus 20:1-17 is meant to be read as an extension of the revelation of God to Israel. The outline and commentary will include vv. 1-20.

I. Introduction (v. 1)
II. Law (vv. 2-17)
    A. Who God is (v. 2)
    B. How to worship God (vv. 3-12)
    C. How to live as the people of God (vv. 13-17)
III. Conclusion (vv. 18-20)

Significance. The primary purpose of the Decalogue is not to provide the people of God with a code of ethics. The list does not contain enough commands to provide a comprehensive rule for living. In addition, the larger narrative context suggests that the Decalogue is better read as a revelation into the very character of God who is visible on Mount Sinai. When read in this way the purpose of the Decalogue in Exodus 20:1-17 is to tell us that the Torah is a divine gift.

The introduction in v. 1 clarifies the Decalogue because it underscores how law is not a human creation to make knowledge of God more manageable, but divine revelation that seeks to transform me or you.

The body of laws in vv. 2-17 are structured to underscore the point of the introduction. The laws are introduced in v. 2 with a divine self-revelation that is meant to put content into the character of God as savior. The God on Mount Sinai is the power that was behind the Exodus. The remainder of the Decalogue provides a structure whereby Israel can claim the salvific power of God and thus allow this power to descend from the mountaintop through their worship and ultimately into their communal life.

This imagery of a divine descent underscores how worship must be the central channel for claiming God's power, since it is the link between God on the mountaintop and Israel below. Not surprisingly, therefore, worship and how we imagine God in it are the focus for the first four laws in vv. 3-12. The divine power of salvation is (1) not transferable to anything else, (2) cannot be contained in any object, (3) is a power that is potent and dangerous in our world, thus the name of the God of the Exodus should not be used casually, and (4) is available in worship. The final laws make a strong statement that the divine power of salvation must not be restricted to worship, but must also transform all communal activity. The final six laws illustrate the point by making reference to (5) honoring parents, (6) not killing, (7) not committing adultery, (8) not stealing, (9) not lying, and (10) not coveting. In particular, the structure of the Decalogue is important even if it is not exhaustive. It does not move from social activity to God, rather it moves from God to social activity, and the key to this latter structure is worship. Worship is where we receive revelation that can be translated into law, which can then restructure our lives.

The conclusion in vv. 18-20 underscores the point made in the introduction and in the structure of the laws, which is that the Decalogue is best read as revelation and not simply as a code of ethics. The imagery of lightning and thunder in v. 18 is a description of theophany (the appearance of God). The shift back to theophany in v. 18 suggests that the very hearing of the Decalogue in vv. 2-17 was the equivalent of seeing God as thunder and lightning. This conclusion is reinforced by the motif of the fear of the people, which is a common reaction when God appears to someone. The description of the people fearing God in v. 18 can apply to both the theophany of lightning and the revelation of law. The conclusion to be drawn from this close linking of theophany and law with the motif of fear is that fear of the law is fear of God. And, in v. 20, we are told that this fear is a good thing, because it will keep our lives pure. This conclusion is echoed in Psalm 19.

The Response: *Psalm 19*

In Praise of the Law

Setting. Psalm 19 is composed of two apparently distinct psalms. Verses 1-6 are a hymn that praises the power of God in creation. Verses 7-14 shift the focus from nature as a source of revelation to the law. The praise of law as a source of revelation is a fitting complement to the revelation of the Decalogue in Exodus 20:1-20.

Structure. The focus of interpretation will be on the second part of the psalm—vv. 7-14. Psalm 19:7-14 separates into two or three parts, depending on whether v. 14 stands alone or is included with vv. 11-13. The following outline will divide the psalm between the praise of law in vv. 7-10 and a prayer of supplication in vv. 11-14.

    I. The Praise of Divine Power in Creation (vv. 1-6)
   II. The Praise of Law (vv. 7-10)
      A. The power of the law to transform persons (vv. 7-8)
      B. A summary
         1. Influence of law on persons (v. 9*a*)
         2. The value of law (vv. 9*b*-10)
  III. Prayer of Supplication (vv. 11-14)
      A. Request for revelation (vv. 11-13)
      B. Rededication (v. 14)

Significance. The imagery that is associated with the law in vv. 7-10 and the request of the psalmist for revelation in order to understand the law in vv. 11-13 make it clear that law must not be understood in legalistic terms. As was the case with the Decalogue, law is understood to be revelation that can actually transform a person. Note how the law is contrasted with different parts of the psalmist's body in vv. 7-8. The law that is perfect, sure, right, and pure can transform the psalmist by giving back life, bestowing wisdom, rejuvenating the heart, and enlightening the eyes. The result of the transforming power of the law on the psalmist is stated in v. 9*a*. It results in an enduring fear of God. This is the same imagery as Exodus 20:18-20. Verses 9*b*-10 conclude that law is more valuable than gold, because it is able to instill permanent fear in the people of God.

In this section the law is not clear; revelation is required for our understanding. We are far removed from the cut-and-dry world of legalism in these verses, and much closer to the setting of the divine revelation on Mount Sinai from Exodus 20:1-17. The praise of law in vv. 7-10 prompts the psalmist to request its power in vv. 11-13 and then to rededicate a pursuit of the life of faith in v. 14.

New Testament Texts

The lessons take exception to two different erroneous assumptions about valid religion and assert the definitive place of Jesus Christ in God's involvement with humanity. The epistle text denies the idea that human knowledge is the key to correct Christian living, and the Gospel lesson rejects the notion that human practices, even with the most extraordinarily stringent standards, can qualify us as necessarily acceptable to God. In other words, we find warnings against becoming puffed up or overly confident because of our thoughts or our activities. Instead, both texts identify God's work in Jesus Christ as the locus of saving grace.

The Epistle: *I Corinthians 1:18-25*

God's Extraordinary Ways

Setting. The verses of the lesson come early in the body of Paul's first letter to the Corinthians. Having declared in the opening of the main portion of the letter that elegant proclamation may indeed empty the cross of Christ of its true power (1:17), Paul moves in this passage to meditate on the striking, even peculiar (from a human point of view), manner in which God wrought salvation for humankind. From this point Paul will turn to the Corinthians, using their own backgrounds as evidence of the veracity of his claims, all the while seeking to divert their attention away from themselves (the cause of controversy behind the writing of this letter) and toward God (the source of salvation).

Structure. In v. 18 Paul articulates his thesis, which he justifies through the quotation of Scripture (1:19). Then, in vv. 20-25 Paul employs various rhetorical strategies—questions, declarations, juxtapositions—to emphasize that God's ways, though unexpected, are superior. The variety of styles in Paul's deliberations invites creativity in the development of the sermon.

Significance. Paul teaches that God works in direct defiance of human standards. Moreover, God's work is powerful, so that it incapacitates and reverses the established values of this world. Paul declares this as fact and argues to establish his case.

Verse 18 is an arresting statement, articulating one of Paul's central theological convictions. Paul says (I have translated and schematized the statement),

> "For the word of the cross
> (A) to the ones who are perishing
> (B) is folly;
> but
> (A´) to us who are being saved
> (B´) it is the power of God."

He contrasts two groups: (1) those who are perishing and (2) those who are being saved; and he numbers himself and the Corinthians in the latter group. The criterion for the separation of these groups is the cross—specifically the word (that is, the preaching) of the cross. The cross has different meaning for the groups. To those who are perishing it is folly, but to those being saved it is (one would expect in the structural juxtapositions of Paul's remark to read "the wisdom of God," but instead one finds) the power of God. This is the apostle's "theology of the cross." Paul deliberately shapes a remark to drive home the point that the cross is the power of God that saves a group of humans. In other words, Paul argues that it is not human activity—even as a comprehending of God's ways—but divine action that saves humanity.

Paul backs up his point with a quotation of Isaiah 29:14, and he uses the verb *thwart* rather than the verb *conceal*, which actually occurs in the Septuagint. In short, Paul modifies the text to make it more applicable to his argument. His point is to give scriptural precedent for God's work in the cross of Christ, not merely to provide a prooftext. Paul's use of the Bible shows that Scripture is absolutely authoritative, essential, and of penultimate significance. The text serves "the word of the cross," and the preacher's ultimate concern is with the gospel, not the text.

In the following verses, Paul jabs at those who may differ with his teaching. He asks after the wise, the scribe, and the debater "of this age." His phrase, "of this age," locates where human wisdom originates. Then, Paul talks about what God has done in and through the crucified Christ. Paul's argument contends that humans do not rea n their way to God, because God saves by the (word of) the cross of Christ which, by this world's standards, is "folly." The point: Salvation is God's activity. Preaching Christ as crucified brings a crisis of separation. To deny God's saving work shows bondage to "this world"; whereas, those who believe the gospel are called, which shows they are grasped by the power of God. Believers know the crucified Christ as God's wisdom.

Verse 25 ends this section with an epigrammatic truth that Paul applies to the Corinthian situation in the following verses (26-31). Worldly wisdom judges the wisdom of God to be foolishness; but, in fact, the supposed foolishness of God renders worldly wisdom into true foolishness. Thus, one sees the power of the wisdom of God. Behind the argument is the conviction that salvation is purely the work of God. Should human reasoning or activity be the source of salvation, then some humans would surely have an advantage over others and none would have need for God. But salvation is not a human achievement, and the gospel declares that God's saving power levels human distinctions and comes to all as grace.

The Gospel: *John 2:13-22*

The Work and Words of Jesus as Signs of God's Will and Power

Setting. There are two stories in the second chapter of John—Jesus at a wedding and Jesus in the Temple. These reports could have existed separately and independently (see the other Gospels which recall the Temple incident but do not tell of the wedding), but John placed them back-to-back. The Fourth Gospel tells us certain activities of Jesus were "signs"—that is, manifestations of Jesus' glory meant to bring people to belief (see 2:11 and 20:30-31). The Synoptic Gospels recall Jesus' radical acts in the Temple toward the very end of their accounts of Jesus' ministry, but John places the same story near the beginning of Jesus' work and adjacent to the story of the sign done at the wedding in Cana of Galilee. The two stories in John 2 are set so that they interpret each other. Now, from the start of John's account of Jesus' ministry through the correlation of theses two incidents we clearly know Jesus and that for which he stands.

Structure. There are three major components in vv. 13-25. The story is formed in such a way that it supports and presents these three elements. First, there is the action itself of Jesus' disrupting business in the Temple. Second, there is the questioning of Jesus' authority. And, third, there is the mysterious saying about the Temple.

Significance. What is Jesus' protest about? The story gives us clues for interpretation. Jesus' dramatic show of disapproval is a radical criticism of the Temple cult and its sacrificial system that is quite similar to the severe critiques that were regularly offered by Old Testament prophets (see, for example, Jeremiah 7:1-14, and notice the quotation in 2:17 of Psalm 69:9 which interprets the action). Jesus' words in this account (2:16) seem to be an allusion to Zechariah 14:21. The statement implies that Jesus objected to the grandiose show of piety that insisted on pure animals and coins while failing to insist upon corresponding purity of heart. Moreover, Jesus seems concerned with the purity or sanctity of the place itself, for it is a holy place that is God's, which should symbolize the divine not the human traffic in the name of and at the expense of the divine.

Jesus' adversaries throughout the Gospel, the Jews (an odd reference since Jesus himself, his disciples, and the great majority of the characters who appear in the Gospel are all Jews), inquire what proof ("sign") he can offer for the authenticity of his actions. What authorized Jesus to do what he did? Jesus does not answer the inquiry directly. Typical of his words and deeds in the Fourth Gospel Jesus makes a statement in response to the challenge that eludes the comprehension of those with whom he converses. There is a strangely satirical dimension to Jesus' declaration. Indeed, the Temple of which

44

he spoke, his body, was "destroyed," and, indeed, he was raised from the dead; but the Temple of which his challengers assumed he spoke was also destroyed in 70 B.C.E. by the Romans, and to this day it has not been rebuilt. The irony identifies the great difference between divine power and human impotence. The manner in which Jesus states his enigmatic reply heightens this contrast, "You do this, and I'll do that." Divine power is superior to human capacity to the point that it can and does undo seditious human action. Yet frequently humans do not even have the ability to reverse their own acts.

By speaking of the Resurrection here at the outset of Jesus' ministry the Fourth Gospel reveals a number of significant things to its readers. First, from the start of his ministry Jesus both knows and controls his own fate. As the Son of God his authority is that of divine power, and we hear in his assertion the truth of God's sovereignty and presence in and through Jesus Christ. Second, we learn of our finite capacities as humans. The words should humble us. The humility we are called to exhibit is humility in relation to God, and it is meant to instill genuine appreciation of God and to foster an appropriate relationship between Creator and creatures. Third, we learn of the vulnerability of God through Jesus Christ. We do not hear, "You can't touch me!" Rather, Christ's words disclose the degree of God's openness to humankind, yet they do not relinquish God's ultimate authority.

God's vulnerability through Jesus Christ

Lent 3: The Celebration

The rehearsal of the Ten Commandments at the beginning of the liturgy has been a long tradition in many English-speaking churches since the sixteenth century. That has disappeared with the introduction of services that are less penitential in character, but it is certainly appropriate for Lenten worship, and the loss of it altogether would be a denial of the Decalogue as gift as described in the foregoing exegetical remarks. Many congregations may still remember (or practice) the custom of rehearsing the Decalogue with the sung response, "Lord, have mercy upon us, and incline our hearts to keep this law," or, if they were grouped together, "Lord, have mercy upon us, and write all these Thy laws in our hearts, we beseech Thee." The responses may still be found in the service music of many hymnals.

The *Alternative Service Book 1980* of the Church of England has included a form of the Decalogue that pairs each of the commandments with a passage from the New Testament.

Minister: Our Lord Jesus Christ said, If you love me, keep my commandments; happy are those who hear the word of God and keep it. Hear then these commandments which God has given to his people, and take them to heart. I am the Lord your God: you shall have no other gods but me. You shall love the Lord your God with all your heart, with all your soul, with all your mind, and with all your strength.

All: Amen. Lord, have mercy.

Minister: You shall not make for yourself any idol. God is spirit, and those who worship him must worship in spirit and in truth.

All: Amen. Lord, have mercy.

Minister: You shall not dishonor the name of the Lord your God. You shall worship him with awe and reverence.

All: Amen. Lord, have mercy.

Minister: Remember the Lord's day and keep it holy. Christ is risen from the dead: set your minds on things that are above, not on things that are on the earth.

All: Amen. Lord, have mercy.

Minister: Honor your father and mother. Live as servants of God; honor everyone; love the people of God.

All: Amen. Lord, have mercy.

Minister: You shall not commit murder. Be reconciled to your neighbor; overcome evil with good.

All: Amen. Lord, have mercy.

Minister: You shall not commit adultery. Know that your body is a temple of the Holy Spirit.

All: Amen. Lord, have mercy.

Minister: You shall not steal. Be honest in all that you do and care for those in need.

All: Amen. Lord, have mercy.

Minister: You shall not be a false witness. Let everyone speak the truth.

All: Amen. Lord, have mercy.

Minister: You shall not covet anything which belongs to your neighbor. Remember the words of the Lord Jesus: It is more blessed to give than to receive. Love your neighbor as yourself, for love is the fulfilling of the law.

All: **Amen. Lord, have mercy.**

This reading should be followed by a time for silent recollection and confession and then by words of forgiveness or assurance of pardon pronounced by the pastor. The use of this as a form for confession does not preclude the reading of the lesson from Exodus in the usual place for the Old Testament lesson in the service. In fact, there may be value in having the text reinforced by its appearance in two guises, especially since it seems to be so rarely heard anywhere anymore.

Fourth Sunday in Lent

Old Testament Texts

Numbers 21:4-9 is the story of how Israel was attacked by snakes in the wilderness, and then saved by the construction of a bronze serpent. Psalm 107:1-3, 17-22 is a hymn of praise.

The Lesson: *Numbers 21:4-9*

The Bronze Serpent

Setting. Numbers 21:4-9 is a murmuring story. A murmuring story is meant to accentuate the tendency of Israel to complain throughout their wilderness journey. They are hardly in the wilderness before they complain to Moses about water (Exodus 15:22-27; 17:1-7) and food (Exodus 16). Murmuring stories give way in Exodus 19 through Numbers 10 as Israel receives revelation from God on Mount Sinai. But this genre returns once Israel resumes their journey in Numbers 11. There are six murmuring stories in Numbers 11–21 (11:1-3, 11:4-34, 13–14, 16–17, 20:1-3, 21:4-9), of which 21:4-9 is the last.

Structure. The murmuring stories follow the same pattern in structure. In the earliest stories they begin with a situation of crisis over the lack of water or food. Israel complains to Moses about the situation, prompting Moses to intercede, which results in a divine response. This pattern evolves into stronger confrontations between God and Israel after the revelation of Sinai. Numbers 21:4-9 presents the culmination of this development. Although the stereotyped pattern is still discernible, the situation of crisis is no longer clear. Verse 4 simply states that the people became impatient, while their actual complaint in v. 5 is that they don't like what their eating. Furthermore, v. 5 underscores how Israel's complaint goes beyond Moses to include

48

God, which prompts divine punishment in the form of fiery snakes. Divine punishment, however, induces confession of sin by Israel, intercession by Moses, and a response by God (vv. 7-8) instructing Moses to construct a bronze serpent, which contains the power to heal when gazed upon by Israelites.

Significance. Two aspects of Numbers 21:4-9 must be underscored in preaching this text. First, even though snakes are mentioned as being a menace in the wilderness (Isaiah 30:6), the incident in Numbers 21:4-9 should not be read as a story about a natural hazard. Rather the snakes are a divine response to Israel's sin of complaining. The snakes, therefore, represent divine punishment, and they may, themselves, have mythological characteristics. What the NRSV translates as in vv. 6 and 8 as "poisonous serpents" is literally "seraph serpents," which may translate "fiery serpents" (whatever that means) or may simply be left untranslated, in which case the word might also refer to a six-winged mythological creature. The exact meaning is unclear. Second, what is clear is that the "bronze serpent" in v. 9 represents an antidote to the deadly bite of the seraph serpents. Serpents, therefore, acquire two functions in the text. They represent both divine punishment and divine healing. The function of the bronze snake to heal appears to have roots in the Jerusalem cult, where Nehushtan, the bronze serpent, seems to have had a long history. This serpent was removed by Hezekiah (II Kings 18:4).

The use of Numbers 21:4-9 in reference to Jesus apparently emphasizes the atoning function of the bronze servant, and perhaps this is the aspect of the text that should be clarified for preaching. Atonement is misinterpreted, however, if it develops into a topical sermon and is explained independently of the larger murmuring cycle, in which divine punishment is the first response to Israel's sin. Only with this context firmly fixed does the radical nature of atonement—as unexpected healing—acquire meaning.

The Response: *Psalm 107:1-3, 17-22*

Giving Thanks

Setting. Psalm 107 separates into at least two parts. Verses 1-32 are a song of thanksgiving, and vv. 33-43 are a mixture of hymnic praise and wisdom sayings. The first section appears to have a liturgical setting of praise in which a priest would have called a congregation to praise (v. 1) by providing four different situations in which the salvation of God could have been experienced by the worshipers (vv. 4-32). The four situations included those who traveled the desert and experienced the deliverance of God through food and direction (vv. 4-9), those hopelessly lost in prison who experienced the presence of God (vv. 10-16), those who were sick and recovered (vv. 17-22), and, finally, those who traveled the dangerous seas and experienced God's salvation by surviving a storm (vv. 23-32). The second part of the psalm (vv. 33-43) is meant to provide still more occasions of salvation that prompt praise to God.

Structure. The lectionary text separates into three parts: an introductory call to praise in v. 1, perhaps an extension of the call to praise in vv. 2-3, and the experience of divine help in a time of sickness in vv. 17-22.

Significance. The central imagery in using Psalm 107 as a response is the motif of giving thanks to God in a situation of need.

New Testament Texts

The lessons—Ephesians 2:1-10 and John 3:14-21—ponder the means and the meaning of salvation. Both texts declare the saving work of God in Jesus Christ, and they reflect upon the significance of this work for the quality of human life, both now and in the future.

The Epistle: *Ephesians 2:1-10*

What It Means to Be a Believer

Setting. Ephesians seems unrelated to any specific situation, but it is clearly concerned with every divine and human moment. The epistle falls into two broad parts: chapters 1–3 are an elaborate, profoundly theological statement. Almost esoteric in nature, they are lofty, complex, and even elegant. Chapters 4–6 are still elevated in style, expression, and outlook, but here we find statements about the ordering of the everyday life of believers. The theme of this epistle, in both its theological and practical parts, is cosmic reconciliation.

The first twenty-two verses of chapter 1 are focused on the individual believer, and only at v. 23 does the author introduce the Church as the universal body of Christ. Yet, to prevent one from moving from the level of the individual believer to that of the Church universal and, in turn, forgetting the crucial implications of salvation for the individual members of the body, the author drops back in 2:1-10 to contrast the pitiful life without Christ to the glories of life brought by the power of Christ's salvation.

Structure. The reflection in these verses is elevated, but the logic is progressive and clear. The lesson articulates the substance of salvation, ponders the way that salvation comes to the believer and the way it does not, and declares that to which salvation leads. The path of the logic is from salvation to the individual believer to the life of the Church. Thus, while salvation is the overarching theme, the verses meditate on both the individual and corporate dimensions of salvation and the relationship between the two.

Significance. The heart of this passage is a contrast between the gloomy predicament of a human life lived without Christ and the gracious glories of life lived in his healing resurrection power. Having mentioned the Church (1:23, "his body"), the author's mind recoils to the individual believer. A reader could conclude that the bounteous benefits of faith are found through merely joining the Church, but the author undermines such faulty logic. For Ephesians the Church is the corporate community of saved individuals. Unless salvation has meaning for the individual, there is nothing personal or compelling about the experience of Christ. Yet clearly individuals do not simply derive benefits from attaching themselves to the Church. Rather, the only legitimate way to become a member of the Church is to be a believer. Church membership does not make one a Christian. We are Christians through our individual and personal experiences.

Yet Christianity is not individualism. Being a Christian means, in turn, affiliation with and participation in the life of the Church—Ephesians makes this plain; but the lesson labors to make sure that readers do not miss the individual meaning of salvation through artificially focusing on the meaning of Church membership. As believers, we neither stand alone nor hide in the Church; rather, we are individuals mutually related to one another through our unique relationships to Christ as individual believers. The vertical dimension of faith is the source and power of the horizontal dimension of life in Christ. In part Christian life for individual Christians means that because of personal relationships to Christ, we are led to become members of the corporate body of Christ.

Beyond this crucial basic matter, three striking themes in this text require recognition and, perhaps, treatment in proclamation. First, the difference between life before and life after Christ is the difference between life and death, now and forever. This is a matter of the quality of life as well as the energy or enduring value of life. Second, the transformation of life, from death to life, comes through the believer's relationship to Christ himself and comes by the grace of God. The experience of salvation, meaning the real transformation of existence, is the work of God. The text tells the good news of God's saving grace in Christ, and it bluntly puts believers in their proper places (see vv. 8-9). Third, in expressing the truly inexpressible character of Christian life, Ephesians draws on the story of Christ himself to explicate the meaning of salvation for the believer. The author goes farther than any other New Testament writer in using the story of Christ for declaring the glories of Christian life. Believers have died with Christ, they are raised with Christ, and they are exalted with Christ into the heavenly places. This manner of speaking may seem to expound a purely realized eschatology, but notice there is a future that is open to, but different from, the present; indeed, the future is anticipated as greater than the present (v. 7).

The Gospel: *John 3:14-21*

"For God So Loved the World"

Setting. John 3:1-21 is the account of Jesus' encounter with Nicodemus. The section follows on the reference in 2:23-25 to the signs Jesus did when he went to Jerusalem for the festival. It was the signs that brought Nicodemus to him to inquire about his identity. The verses of the lesson are a final statement by Jesus, which conclude a series of exchanges between him and Nicodemus. The statements in the lesson are not dependent on the previous remarks for intelligibility, so the detachment of vv. 14-21 from the foregoing scene causes no problems for using these verses in worship; but understanding their place in and relation to the remainder of the scene is helpful.

Structure. The story in John 3 is clearly patterned. After the narrative introduction and initial declaration by Nicodemus in vv. 1-2, there are three cycles of exchanges between Jesus and Nicodemus. First, Jesus makes a pronouncement in v. 3 that leads to a question by Nicodemus in v. 4. Second, Jesus makes another pronouncement (vv. 5-8) and Nicodemus asks another question (v. 9). And, third, Jesus begins to make a final pronouncement in v. 11, which continues perhaps through v. 21 (although Jesus' remarks may end after v. 15, so that vv. 16-21 are commentary from the author of the Gospel).

Significance. The third statement by Jesus to Nicodemus (vv. 11-21) is concerned with the role of Jesus in salvation. After Jesus' amazing pronouncement, notice there is no response by Nicodemus. In fact, we find that Nicodemus has completely dropped out of the story, to appear again only in chapter 7 (and later in chapter 19). For the verses of our lesson, Nicodemus is less than a presupposition, although the previous two pronouncements by Jesus to Nicodemus set the scene for this final statement. Initially Jesus spoke about the necessity of divinely empowered spiritual birth and, then, about entry into the kingdom of God based entirely on that godly rejuvenation.

The lesson teaches that at God's initiative, because of God's love, God sent (or gave) God's own Son. The Son, Jesus Christ, is the criterion for salvation. In the sending of Christ, God precipitated a crisis—in Jesus' very person and presence. This crisis separates (a) light from dark and (b) truth from evil—(a´) faith from unbelief and (b´) those humans on God's side from those set in opposition to God. The presence of Jesus brings forth the issue whether one is for or against him (and God). There is no middle position, so that the person of Jesus becomes the standard for distinguishing and judging between humans.

With the separation enacted, we learn that the death of Jesus is the basis for the salvation given to those who are aligned on God's side through faith in Jesus Christ. The lesson maintains that belief is the absolutely necessary condition for experiencing saving grace. We also learn that the object of belief is Jesus, the Son of God, and that the corollary of belief is a life lived in doing the truth. There is an inseparable bonding of correct belief (in God's Son, Jesus, as the agent of salvation) and correct living (according to God's will as expressed in the teaching of Jesus Christ). In other words, mere orthodoxy is not the key to Christian existence; rather, the center of Christian reality is an inseparable bonding of orthodoxy and orthopraxis.

To put the matter in another way and from a slightly different angle, "eternal life" is a quality of existence that has its beginning in this life in full anticipation of another life. Eternal life is actual (more than possible!) because of what God has done in Jesus Christ, and the Christian lives out of a belief in Jesus that empowers and guides all of existence. Because our lives are renewed through faith in Jesus Christ, we are in touch with the will and the work of God. God's will is sufficient to effect the transformation of our existence, both now and in God's future. As our lives are invested in Jesus Christ, through belief, God's power manifested in Christ grasps us and holds us in the security of God's own grip.

Proclamation that treats the theme of "eternal life," which is prominent in this lesson, should notice several items: Eternal life is, on the one hand, life after death in the presence of God; but, on the other hand, this life, God's greatest gift to humanity, is God's own life. Because of the cross of Christ, eternal life is not restricted to the future but is equally related to current living. Eternal life is a thoroughgoing relationship to God in and through belief in Jesus Christ who himself brings the life of God into the lives of humans, now and forever.

Lent 4: The Celebration

The Old Testament lesson for today was chosen to correspond to the Gospel lesson's reference to the serpent in the wilderness. An understanding of atonement as healing might be explored by means of this image.

Each of the lessons require that the preacher give some attention to the doctrine of the atonement and how best to interpret it in clear and relevant ways for modern hearers. Obviously, this means that preachers must be clear themselves as to what they mean by atonement and its place for them in their own systematic theology. The preaching of the atonement usually illustrates how much theological bias a preacher brings to a particular text, because there is a demonstrable tendency to interpret Scriptures in the light of our prior understanding of atonement rather than the other way around.

Preparation for preaching this Sunday provides a rationale for locking ourselves in the study and spending several rigorous hours both pouring over theological works that may have been collecting dust since seminary days and discovering some later works that may have other insights to challenge and stimulate our exegetical and homiletical abilities. Here, then, is a bibliography of works on the atonement intended to be representative of various points of view across the theological horizon. Some acquaintance with as many of them as possible will protect the preacher from prejudging the scriptural texts too quickly.

Gustaf Aulen's *Christus Victor* (New York: Macmillan, 1961) is a classic text that discusses three main types of atonement theory. Most readers will have related to one or another of them at some time (and may still be trying to find alternatives to them!). Donald Baillie's *God Was in Christ* (London: Faber & Faber, 1948) represents one of the finest attempts by a twentieth-century theologian to reinterpret the doctrine in a way that holds in balance a concern for the integrity of the historical Jesus and the content of the apostolic testimony. These two volumes can serve as an introduction and interpretive guide for these other entries in our minimalist bibliography on the atonement.

The Atonement and the Social Process by Shailer Mathews (New York: Macmillan, 1930) is no longer in print, but it is well worth the hunt. It represents an early modernist interpretation that will have a contemporary ring to those who have read much in liberation theology. A later neoorthodox perspective is ably stated in John Driver's *Understanding the Atonement for the Mission of the Church* (Scottdale, Penn.: Herald Press, 1986).

An evangelical interpretation is to be found in Donald G. Bloesch's impressive work, *God, Authority, and Salvation,* vol. 1 of *Essentials of Evangelical Theology* (San Francisco: Harper & Row, 1978).

Norman Pittenger outlines a process view in *Freed to Love: A Process Interpretation of Redemption* (Wilton, Conn.: Morehouse-Barlow, 1987). Thomas Oden, in the second volume of his systematic theology, *The Word of Life* (San Francisco: Harper & Row, 1989) makes a case for an interpretation of atonement based primarily upon a re-examination of the writings of theologians, both women and men, from the early centuries.

Fifth Sunday in Lent

Old Testament Texts

Jeremiah 31:31-34 sketches out a vision of a new covenant. Psalm 51:1-12 is a petitionary prayer for forgiveness.

The Lesson: *Jeremiah 31:31-34*

What Is New About the New Covenant?

Setting. Jeremiah 31:31-34 has had a long and prominent history in Christian interpretation starting with the writer of Hebrews, who presents a christological midrash on this text in chapters 8 and 10. According to this author the answer to the question of what is new in Jeremiah 31:31-34 is Jesus. Jesus is the new covenant and this fact has implications for divine forgiveness and Christian worship. The christological interpretation of Jeremiah is a powerful insight into the text, especially when preaching Hebrews 8 and 10. A problem arises, however, when we too quickly use Hebrews to interpret Jeremiah 31:31-34, since both the social context and the theological horizons of this latter text are very different. In view of this, we must bracket momentarily our tendency to interpret the new covenant in Jeremiah 31:31-34 as a prediction of Jesus, so that we can ask the question: What is new about covenant in Jeremiah? An answer to this question may provide insight into why the author of Hebrews chose to quote the entire text of Jeremiah 31:31-34 in trying to provide commentary on the mission of Jesus.

Structure. The phrase, "Thus says the Lord," provides a clue to the structure of Jeremiah 31:31-34. It occurs four times, once in each verse, which suggests that the text be outlined into four parts. Verse 31 provides an eschatological setting for the discourse on the new covenant. What follows, therefore, is a utopian vision that includes both the northern and the southern kingdoms. This is the only place in the Old Testament where the word "new" is used to describe covenant. Verse 32 provides initial contrast between the old and new covenants by describing what the new covenant will not be. It is not the covenant of the Exodus which is characterized by two things: disobedience of Israel and God's role as master (Hebrew, *ba'al*—compare the translation "master" with "husband" in the NRSV). Verse 33 switches from the past to provide the content of the new covenant. It will be characterized by the internalization of the law into the very character of Israel, with the result that the Lord will be God and Israel the people of God. Finally, v. 34 sketches out the results of the new covenant. All will know God and God will forgive.

Significance. The newness of covenant in Jeremiah 31:31-34 does not consist in any of the specific elements listed. The internalization of Torah or law within the hearts of Israel is not really new, since the law was always meant to be internalized (see Deuteronomy 30:6), and God's ability to forgive is not a new divine attribute, since this quality was already firmly in place at the time of the Exodus (see Exodus 32). Rather the newness of the covenant consists in the surprising reversals that are referred to in these few verses.

Scholars debate when Jeremiah 31:31-34 was written. Some attribute the text to the prophet, Jeremiah, himself, during the closing days of the monarchy, while others locate it in the late exile or early post-exilic period, in which case the writer may be part of later deuteronomistic tradition, which was idealizing the prophet at that time. In either case, the vision of an unexpected new covenant creates tensions with the traditional understanding of covenant in the Book of Deuteronomy. The language looks to be deuteronomistic (emphasis on Exodus, Torah, the heart, covenant, and so on), but it does not conform to the covenant theology of Deuteronomy. At the center of the tension is the belief in deuteronomistic tradition that covenant is conditional upon obedience. What this means is that God is obligated to Israel only insofar as they adhere to the covenantal stipulations. Jeremiah 11 reflects this deuteronomistic understanding of covenant. The point of Jeremiah 11 is that because Israel has broken covenant,

God does not want to hear any prayers or petitions for help. The covenant has been broken and God is now free of all obligations, with the result that Israel will lose the land and go into exile. With such an understanding of covenant, there really is no place for eschatology once the contract is broken, which means that Jeremiah 31:31-34 should not be in the book. But there it is.

The literary context of Jeremiah 31:31-34 accentuates its inappropriateness with regard to the orthodox understanding of covenant in deuteronomistic tradition, because it has been placed squarely in the setting of the fall of the southern kingdom, which is the fulfillment of Jeremiah 11 and thus the end of covenant. There are two ways to read the passage, once the paradoxical setting has been noted. One way is to read it solely as a statement about a utopian future, which is disconnected from anything in the past. The newness of the covenant in this case is not a transformation of tradition, but the beginning of new tradition. This understanding of the passage is frequently used in Christian interpretation to talk about Jesus, the new beginning. Another way to read the passage is to bring it in conversation with the orthodox understanding of covenant in deuteronomistic tradition. When read in this way the emphasis on newness is not an attempt to escape the past/present by constructing a utopian future, but the aim is to evaluate critically past orthodoxy because of its power to predetermine what are the limits of God's obligations and acts of salvation. When viewed in this way, what the passage is saying is that God can make a new covenant even though it is not in the theological blueprint of Israel. God can perform surprising reversals.

Both of the readings listed above are essential for interpreting Jeremiah 31:31-34, but there is a logical order to them. The initial focus for interpreting the new covenant within the context of the Book of Jeremiah must be the critique of orthodoxy implied in the text, for it is in this reading that the surprising reversals are felt. If anything was clear at the time of the Exile, with the destruction of the Temple and loss of land, it was that the covenant was no longer in effect. This conclusion was rooted in deep piety: God has rightfully abandoned sinful Israel. Such situations of perceived clarity are the most dangerous for orthodoxy, for they make God too predictable. The new covenant in Jeremiah 31:31-34 undercuts this predictability, and, consequently, it opens up a new and unexpected future with God. The writer of Hebrews saw this characteristic of the text and thus chose it as an avenue to talk about God's unpredictable action in Jesus. The danger for contemporary readers is that what was an unpredictable reversal for the writer of Hebrews has become a well-established orthodoxy. One way to test yourself on whether you have succumbed to the danger of orthodoxy is to check your own reading of Jeremiah 31:31-34. Do you see any surprising reversals here or is it only a future-oriented text that confirms your already established belief in Jesus? The central aim in preaching Jeremiah 31:31-34 is, first, to evaluate critically the orthodoxy of your congregation; and, second, to sketch out new and surprising ways in which God's salvation may be active.

The Response: *Psalm 51:1-12*

A Request for Newness

Setting. Psalm 51 is a radical petitionary prayer for nothing less than an absolutely new beginning. Given the extreme character of the psalm, one can see how it played a central role for Luther and Calvin in constructing their view of the doctrine of justification.

Structure. The boundaries of the lectionary reading separate into several parts. In vv. 1-2 there is petition, followed by confession of guilt in vv. 3-6 and request for forgiveness in vv. 7-9. In vv. 10-12 the psalmist makes a bold request for God to create newness.

Significance. Psalm 51:1-12 provides a powerful complement to Jeremiah 31:31-34 for two reasons. One, the content of the petitionary prayer is a request for the kind of reversal that is being described as a new covenant. From this perspective, the use of the psalm in the worship service allows the congregation to participate in the reversal sketched out by Jeremiah. Second, the strong creation language, underscores how important the power of God as creator becomes in situations of reversal. The opening petition, "Create in me a clean heart O God," employs the most technical word for creation that is used by biblical writers (Hebrew, *bara'*). Only God is the subject of this word, and it is usually reserved to describe the creation of the cosmos (see Genesis 1). Yet when the psalmist petitions for the most radical reversal of all, this word is also employed because only the creator can recreate instantaneously without being encumbered by the past. Jeremiah perceived this when he envisioned a new covenant. Frequently in the contemporary church, images of God as creator are discredited as merely more support for the status quo, while liberationist theologies are then viewed as ideal instruments for change. Psalm 51:1-12 challenges this contemporary consensus about static creation, for it illustrates how the most radical change—instantaneous justification—can be rooted in God's ability to create something new.

New Testament Texts

Both lessons treat Christ's Passion, although differently. Both texts also emphasize Christ's obedience or full dependence upon God's will. Both passages are profoundly christological in cast and articulate a theology of salvation via God's saving work in Jesus Christ.

The Epistle: *Hebrews 5:5-10*

Christ's Suffering, Obedience, and Salvation

Setting. Commentators repeatedly observe that Hebrews begins like a treatise, proceeds like a sermon, and ends like a letter; yet the central sermonic materials that make up the bulk of the writing have an enigmatic philosophical cast unlike most Christian preaching today. The document is a grand meditation on the superior character of the new Christian covenant, designed to undermine any nostalgia for the previous covenant that could motivate a return to former things. In its development Hebrews makes an intimate connection between theological argument and the interpretation of Scripture.

After an introductory section declaring the superiority of Christ over the angels, Hebrews proceeds through several distinguishable divisions to argue its case. Our lesson comes in the second major section, 4:14–7:28, which makes prominent use of Genesis 14 and Psalm 110 to antedate the cultic priesthood with the priesthood of Melchizedek who is presented as the ultimate priestly prototype for

Christ. The thematic context for our lesson is 4:14–5:10 and 7:1-28. The material in 5:11–6:20 is a lengthy excursus urging the readers to progress in theological insight.

Structure. Our lesson begins and ends on the same note: Christ was appointed a priest by God (not by himself or humans) and his priesthood is eternal (see vv. 5-6, 10). In this confessional frame is a three-part meditation on Christ. First, the text recalls Christ's priesthood in terms of prayer, particularly the prayers of his Passion (Gethsemane?). Second, we recall that as the Son of God, Christ suffered and in so doing learned obedience. Third, as the perfect(ed) one, Christ himself is now the source of salvation for all who obey him. As the frame (vv. 5-6, 10) shows, the thought here is unified, but as we note in numbering the thoughts between the sides of the frame, the meditation is dynamic and logically progressive.

Significance. This passage is the second portion of a logical pattern that occurs in other places in Hebrews. First, the author notices the similarities between Jesus Christ and a notable character from the Old Testament; then, he illustrates or argues the superiority of Christ over the figure. Here, vv. 1-4 set up a comparison of Jesus and Aaron, and vv. 5-10 establish the superiority of Christ over Aaron (and all other human priests) by introducing the mysterious figure Melchizedek as a paradigm for Christ. Melchizedek antedated Aaron and received honor from Abraham. The meditation of Hebrews began by comparing Christ and the angels to show Christ's superiority. Later, in 3:1-6 Christ and Moses are compared and contrasted to demonstrate Christ's preeminence. The dynamics of this logic serve two purposes: (1) negatively, it dampens enthusiasm for anyone or anything other than Christ, and (2) positively, it generates confidence in and devotion to Christ. Preaching on the passage should certainly be christocentric.

Moreover, in its meditation on the priesthood of Christ the text develops its christocentric focus in a manner that is suggestive for the content and construction of the sermon. First, in vv. 5-6 we find quotations of Psalm 2:7 and 110:4. Together these citations point to Christ's resurrection-exaltation as a coronation into royal priesthood. The point here is that Christ's office and work are the results of God's work! Christology is crucial, and it ultimately has theological meaning and teaches us about God's saving will and work.

Second, the statement in v. 7 teaches that the entire Passion of Christ functioned as a priestly intercession. Strikingly the language here is the technical vocabulary of sacrificial offering, so that we think of Christ's prayerful Passion as an offering to God, which has the remarkable capacity to save. The idea of atonement is at the heart of this text, and the author thinks of Christ's Passion as a turning to the one who is able to save.

Third, turning to God and fully trusting God is the substance of obedience. Christ's full reliance upon God was "Godly fear" unto salvation. Obedience cannot be reduced to "God wanted Jesus to suffer; he suffered; that's obedience." Rather, in suffering Christ was completely trusting of God alone, and that is obedience. Thus, he modeled faith, but more (as Hebrews would have it), he blazed the path of faith now open to others.

Fourth, as the one perfected through obedient suffering, Jesus Christ is established by God as the source of salvation for all who obey him. In other words, God has made Jesus the very fountainhead of that which he manifested and which he now gives to all who obey him—namely, salvation!

The Gospel: *John 12:20-33*

Seeing Jesus as God Presented Him

Setting. Through the course of his ministry in the Gospel according to John, Jesus attracted a following (although some turned back in offense in John 6). The level of the crowd's enthusiasm was greatly raised by Jesus' raising of Lazarus in John 11 (see 11:45), as was the hostility toward Jesus on the part of the Jewish leaders (see 11:46-53). Jesus' public ministry comes to its conclusion in John 12 as Jesus enters Jerusalem in a deluge of praise and consternation (12:12-19). The Pharisees express dismay that "the world has gone after him" (12:19). The verses of our lesson begin by telling of the coming of some Greeks to see Jesus and, in turn, recall a series of statements and reactions relating to Jesus' forthcoming Passion.

Structure. The text finds its structure in the unfolding series of statements, reactions, and responses. Greeks come to see Jesus who recognizes immediately that their coming signals the end of his public ministry. Jesus speaks past the point at hand, commenting and praying about his Passion. God responds to Jesus, but the crowd cannot understand. Jesus speaks further, and because the crowd continues to be confused, he and they engage in conversation that lays out his destiny and its meaning (although the crowd never understands). Themes at the heart of this passage include "curiosity about Christ," "Christ's purposefulness," "Christ's complete trust in God," "God's affirmation of Jesus," "the saving significance of Jesus' death," and "Christ as God's saving presence." No single sermon can exhaust this text, so the proclamation should strive for substance, simplicity, and balance.

Significance. One approach to this striking and complex text is to notice the balance struck between the coming of the Greeks and the statements made by Jesus. It is their arrival that signals the arrival of his hour. As Greeks are drawn to Jesus, in whatever kind of curiosity, he recognizes that the time has come for the end of his historical mission to the house of Israel. The language in Jesus' recognition of the time is rich. His hour is the time of his death and resurrection; it is also the time of his glorification, which means his return to his heavenly Father who sent him into the world. The process of his glorification is cast in terms of bearing fruit. Through his death and resurrection he plants a seed that ripens in the hearts of humans and ultimately issues in lives of service.

Notice how the Greeks ask to "see" Jesus (v. 21), and notice how he speaks of providing a particular viewing by being "lifted up from the earth" to "draw all people to [himself]" (v. 32). Jesus gives the Greeks a saving showing. The reference to his being lifted up makes a play on both his crucifixion and his subsequent resurrection-exaltation. Jesus presents himself to those wishing to see him and to witness his divine power in a particular way—as the crucified, resurrected, and exalted Son of God. Inherent in this presentation is the crucial identification of the crucified Jesus with the resurrected and exalted Christ. Humans are not given the one without the other. The one crucified is the one God raised and established as Lord, and the Lord is none other than the crucified one. For us to understand God and God's will fully we must hold the crucifixion and resurrection-exaltation together, for to do otherwise is to run the risk of romanticizing suffering or of lapsing into triumphalism. God's glory and power revealed in Jesus Christ are the glory and power of suffering, saving love.

The voice of God in this account underscores this point. God speaks and Jesus hears the words, but the crowd thinks only that an angel has spoken. For the assembled people the voice is given that they may perceive the closeness between the Father and the Son. God's person and will are seen in Jesus Christ. This is the gift of revelation. Yet we are not saved by this information. If we were, Christianity would be gnosticism, wherein correct knowledge about God gives us access to powerful, privileged data that makes us special and above the fray. Our text speaks of light and darkness, seemingly gnostic notions; but it reminds us that the Light came to us as we were in darkness in order to draw us to the Light and to make of us children of Light! God's initiative in salvation is demonstrated in Jesus Christ, and the effect of God's work is that we have a new identity (children of Light) and a transformed existence (we walk in the Light—namely, we live according to God's revealed ways).

Lent 5: The Celebration

Today concludes this Lent's brief summary of covenantal acts into which God entered with Israel by focusing on Jeremiah's vision of a new covenant that God will make. The New Testament lessons then expound on Jesus as the Church's realization of that covenant.

The following prayer from the Uniting Church in Australia picks up several themes and images from today's lessons. It may be used as the opening prayer of the service, or the prayer of the day, just before the reading of the first lesson.

> Hear, O Father, the cry of your Son,
> who, to establish the new and everlasting covenant,
> became obedient to death upon the cross.
> Grant that, through all the trials of this life,
> we may come to share more intimately
> in his redeeming passion;
> and so obtain the fruitfulness of the seed

that falls to the earth and dies,
to be gathered as your harvest for the kingdom.
We ask this through your Son, our Lord Jesus Christ.
(G. T. Ryan, ed., *Sourcebook for Sundays and Seasons 1991*
[Chicago: Liturgy Training Publications, 1990], p. 96.)

Worship planners and preparers of worship bulletins should be encouraged to lay out all unison readings in sense lines like those in the above prayer. It allows for smoother and more understandable reading, particularly if the congregation is not familiar with the text. Those who write prayers for congregational use should test whether or not the prayer is easily rendered in sense lines. The use of sense lines can help check on two things. First, they can monitor whether the prayer does actually make sense, whether the thoughts and images hang together appropriately or not. Second, they can test for adequate pauses for breathing, which are necessary in oral reading. The congregation should not be exhausted at the end of the prayer by the effort needed to keep afloat in a flood of words that runs on and on with no resting place.

An appropriate hymn for today in relation to the Gospel reading is "Lift High the Cross" (Hymnals: Brethren and Mennonite (1992), no. 321; Episcopal, no. 473; Lutheran, no. 377; Ms. Syn. Lutheran, no. 311; 1990 Presbyterian, no. 371; United Methodist, no. 159). Another, out of the gospel song tradition is "Lift Him Up." It may be found in the *AMEC Bicentennial Hymnal,* no. 221; *The Broadman Hymnal,* no. 60; and *Songs of Zion* (Nashville: Abingdon, 1981), no. 59.

"THE GREAT REDEEMING WORK": PRAISE, PRAYER, AND PREACHING IN HOLY WEEK

This week, culminating in the celebration of the Resurrection, is at the heart of the Church's liturgical life, for it gives meaning to all the Church does the rest of the year. It is therefore important that the ordering of public worship and the preparation of sermons be done with a concern for "the basics," for retelling and remembering the story of salvation in such a dynamic fashion that the participants may become aware of their own involvement in God's story.

The posture of the worshiping Church is not that of those who are ignorant of how the story is going to turn out, or of the original disciples as they experienced the horror of the crucifixion and the fear of a similar fate. We do not enter Holy Week ignorant of Easter Day, and that fact informs the character of our celebration. As a recent hymn puts it:

> They could not know, as we do now,
> how glorious is that crown;
> that thorns would flower upon your brow,
> your sorrows heal our own.
> (*The United Methodist Hymnal*, no. 285)

Celebration is still an appropriate word, even for the Good Friday liturgy, because the Church's celebration is always of God's triumph over sin and death, as a sixth-century hymn writer knew:

> Sing, my tongue, the glorious battle,
> sing the ending of the fray;
> now above the cross, the trophy,

sound the loud triumphant lay;
tell how Christ, the world's Redeemer,
as a victim won the day.
(*The United Methodist Hymnal*, no. 296)

Holy Week may be divided into three sections: (1) the Sunday of the Passion, or Palm Sunday; (2) Monday, Tuesday and Wednesday; and (3) the Paschal Triduum [three days] of Maundy Thursday, Good Friday, and Easter Day—which, in its turn, may have the vigil or night service and the service during the day. Because of space limitations, this year's volume will deal only with the lessons of Passion Sunday and Good Friday. The Easter Vigil lessons will be found in the Year A volume, and Maundy Thursday's in Year C. We will discuss the liturgies for all the days of the Triduum, however.

Perhaps the greatest surprise for many in the new structuring of the lectionary and calendar is the changed approach to Palm Sunday, which is now referred to as The Sunday of the Passion or as Passion/Palm Sunday, but not as Palm Sunday only. This means, of course, that the Fifth Sunday in Lent is no longer called Passion Sunday, as it was in the old calendar. It remains simply the Fifth Sunday in Lent. This is to emphasize the centrality of the Passion of Christ in the liturgical celebrations of Holy Week itself and to prepare ourselves more fully for the solemn observance of the Triduum. Palm Sunday, then, is neither a kind of dry run for Easter, nor is it intended to lay all the emphasis upon the triumphal entry in such a way as to allow those who only attend church on Sunday to miss the message of the cross. It is at least Passion/Palm Sunday, reminding us of the reason for the entry into Jerusalem.

Holy Week, by its very character as the time for specific remembering of the events of the Passion, stands out from the rest of Lent. This is accented visually by changing from the purple paraments or the Lenten array to a somber blood-red color for paraments and vestments. Ideally these should be designed for this week in particular, rather than using the same red set as will appear at Pentecost. The red itself should be different in hue, darker than the brighter, red-orange of Pentecost.

The service for Passion/Palm Sunday is divided into two parts. The first is the Entrance Rite (the Liturgy of the Palms), which centers around the narrative of the entry into Jerusalem. This may begin out-of-doors or in the parish hall and then include a procession of all the people into the church for the second major part (the Liturgy of the Passion), which centers around the reading of the Passion narrative from whichever is the controlling Gospel for the year. (The Passion according to St. John is always read on Good Friday.) There should be some obvious contrast between the ''Hosanna's'' of the first part and the ''Crucify!'' of the second. The entry into the church should begin to mark a difference in emphasis as the people prepare to hear the Old Testament lesson. By the conclusion of the service the congregation should be thinking seriously of what it means to spend the ensuing week in the shadow of the cross.

In the event of inclement weather or for some other reason the entire service needs to be done within the church itself, proper planning can still provide for a processional. The choir and minister should enter the chancel in silence and as unobtrusively as possible. When all are in place, then the minister greets the people and offers an appropriate opening prayer. In Year B Mark 11:1-11 is read and then there may be a blessing and distribution of the branches (if they have not been distributed at the door upon arrival). Notice that these should be branches that are waveable. Then, during the singing of such hymns as ''All Glory, Laud, and Honor'' and ''Hosanna, Loud Hosanna,'' the choir leaves the chancel, processes through and around the nave, returning back up the center aisle into the chancel. It is appropriate that the people file out of the pews and process around with the choir. This is liturgical dance at its most basic and most inclusive, since one does not need any sense of rhythm to participate!

Great care needs to be taken in preparing for any dramatic reading of the Passion narrative. Participants should be well-rehearsed. Scripts are available that divide the lesson up into readers' parts. The preparation for this reading may well involve a special Lenten study group as the readers explore the Passion narrative in intensive Bible study. This may be a project for the confirmation class, particularly if its participation and leadership will compensate for having the actual confirmations on this day rather than waiting until the more temporally significant Eastertide.

The lessons for Monday, Tuesday, and Wednesday in Holy Week

are the same all three years of the lectionary cycle. Their intent is not to review the events of the original Holy Week day by day, but to provide the faithful with a context within which to prepare to participate fully in the celebration of the mysteries of our salvation during the Triduum. The Old Testament lessons (Mon., Isaiah 42:1-9; Tue., Isaiah 49:1-7; Wed., Isaiah 50:4-9a) are from the first three servant songs and remind us of the servant character of the Messiah. The epistle lessons (Mon., Hebrews 9:11-15; Tue., I Corinthians 1:18-31; Wed., Hebrews 12:1-3) direct our thoughts to the themes of the cross and atonement. The Gospel readings (Mon., John 12:1-11; Tue., John 12:20-36; Wed., John 13:21-32) serve respectively to identify Jesus as God's anointed, whose death is part of a divine necessity, resulting in the glorification of both God and Christ.

Maundy Thursday is referred to in the Revised Common Lectionary as "Holy Thursday," presumably following the new Roman Catholic usage. A strong case may be made for "Maundy," however, based on the concluding verse of the Gospel (John 13:1-17, 34): "a new commandment I give to you." "Maundy" derives from *mandatum,* the Latin word for "commandment." It is this new commandment that Jesus illustrates at the Last Supper by washing the disciples' feet, which local congregations may observe on this day by the liturgical washing of one another's feet. For congregations that refuse to consider the washing of feet, Heather Murray Elkins has devised a "Liturgy of Basins," which is published in *Sacramental Life* (July/August 1989). The service is based on Jewish hand washing and "offers the means for both corporate and private admission of sin, and assurance of pardon."

The primary emphases of the day are the remembrance of the holy meal that Jesus celebrated with the disciples "on the night in which he was given up for us" (the Last Supper) and thanksgiving for the institution of that holy meal of remembrance through which he has been present with the Church through the ages (the Lord's Supper). The new Roman Catholic practice has been to emphasize the former since they have the feast of Corpus Christi on which to do the latter. Protestant churches, particularly those that celebrate the Lord's Supper only occasionally, can balance these emphases. White paraments rather than passion-red might be more appropriate for this service. Care should be taken not to give the impression of playacting the Last Supper and thus identifying that meal as the only one which informs the meaning of the Lord's Supper. Even on Maundy Thursday this is still the bridal feast of the Lamb and is celebrated by a Church that has had the Emmaus experience. It is purposeful that the lessons for this service do not include any of the synoptic accounts of the Last Supper. What we hear about the Last Supper is from Paul who identifies all later commemorations as eschatological proclamation. The Gospel lesson is from John, who does not describe the actual meal at all. Rather, his emphasis is on the washing of the disciples' feet, with Jesus doing a kind of "show and tell" about the meaning of his ministry.

Planners of worship for Maundy Thursday need to keep in mind the balance between the historical event two thousand years ago and its identification with the Passover experience of Israel, and the present event in which Christ still makes himself available to his people and makes them a sacrament for the world. If the Washing of Feet is observed, it is natural to have it follow the reading of the Gospel and the sermon. Following that, the offertory hymn or anthem should be one of praise and thanksgiving for the gift of Holy Communion. Hymns during Communion should also express joy for the sacrament, rather than being Good Friday/Crucifixion fare. It is after Communion that the aspect of the service changes and the people prepare to recall the suffering and death of Jesus.

Following the prayer after Communion, a versicle and response might be used:

V. And when they had sung a hymn:

R. They went out to the Mount of Olives.

Then, while the congregation sings a hymn such as "'Tis Midnight, and on Olives' Brow," the altar and chancel are stripped of all decoration. The altar cross is veiled in dark red or black, and the people leave in silence.

The Good Friday service should be thought of as a continuation of the Maundy Thursday service. The people return in silence to the setting that they left the night before. The service begins in silence and proceeds quickly to the lessons and the reading of St. John's Passion. This reading may also be done with members of the congregation taking the various parts, the congregation as a whole being the crowd. The sermon today is expected to deal with any of the major themes that emerge from the lessons. The preacher's first task will be to limit carefully how much one sermon can deal with! Additional liturgical resources for today can be found in The Book of Common Prayer and the *New Handbook of the Christian Year*.

Passion Sunday

Old Testament Texts

The Old Testament lessons are very appropriate for Passion Sunday. Isaiah 50:4-9*a* explores the call of the suffering servant, while Psalm 31:9-16 is a lament from the perspective of one who is suffering. As we will see, both of these lessons share a similar three-part structure, which probes the meaning of suffering from somewhat different perspectives.

The Lesson: *Isaiah 50:4-9*a

A Call to Discipleship

Setting. Isaiah 50:4-9*a* is the third of the suffering servant songs (Isaiah 42:1-4[5-9]; 49:1-6; 50:4-9*a*; 52:13–53:12). The first song was the lesson for Epiphany, Year A. Please refer to this lesson for a discussion of the individual and collective interpretations of these songs, because that discussion also applies to our present lesson. In the first servant song (Isaiah 42:1-4[5-9]) God is the primary speaker in declaring the choice of the servant. In the second song (Isaiah 49:1-6) the servant affirms his call from the womb, but then doubts the purpose of it all with the claim that he has labored in vain. This song ends with the divine proclamation that the servant has not labored in vain but is called to be a light to the nations. The lesson for this Passion Sunday is an individual lament (or perhaps better an individual psalm of confidence) by the suffering servant. Here, there is no longer any doubt about the purposefulness of his call. The servant knows that he is called to be God's pupil or disciple no matter what circumstances befall him.

Structure. Isaiah 50:4-9*a* separates into three parts. In vv. 4-5*aa* the servant proclaims his call. This opening section is framed by the phrase, "The Lord God has given me the tongue/has opened my ear. . . ." Verses 5*ab*-6 describe the servant's training in discipleship. The song closes in vv. 7-9*a* with the suffering servant confessing the reliability of God's salvation. This closing unit is framed with the confession, "For the Lord God helps me. . . ."

Significance. The third suffering servant song presents a blueprint for discipleship, for it illustrates how theory and praxis must be one for any follower of God. The opening section of the song in vv. 4-5*aa* roots the authority of the servant in the call of God. In the opening and closing phrase, "The Lord God has, . . ." the servant makes it clear that he has been called to speak for God (the Lord has given him a tongue) and to hear the word of God (the Lord has opened his ear). The servant then tells us that his commissioning to hear God's word is for the purpose of discipleship. We are told in v. 4 that every morning God awakens the servant so that he is able to hear God's instruction like a pupil (Hebrew, *limmudim*; NRSV translation, "to listen as those who are taught"). The second section of the song is marked in v. 5*ab,* when the servant refers to himself and his present situation. In vv. 5*ab*-6 the servant outlines his training in discipleship. Here the work of God is translated into action. The servant does not rebel from God's instruction, but accepts suffering in the present time. The final section (vv. 7-9*a*) shifts the focus back to God and in so doing the servant provides the content of what he has learned as God's disciple, which now allows him to endure suffering. The content of God's tutoring is the proclamation of salvation that frames this unit in vv. 7 and 9 ("The Lord God helps me"). This confession allows for further affirmations about God's salvation by the servant in v. 7 and a direct address to his oppressors in v. 8. In v. 7 the two "therefores" state the servant's resolve to be a disciple, because God is near. In vv. 8-9*a* the servant addresses his opponents through a series of questions: Who will contend with me? Who is my adversary? Who will declare me guilty? The answer, of course, is no one.

The striking thing about this suffering servant song, which must be emphasized in preaching, is how easily it moves between the images of student and suffering activist, between knowing the content of salvation in the classroom and doing the work of salvation. Neither theory nor praxis is allowed a special role over the other in the servant's soliloquy on discipleship. The servant is able to endure suffering because he knows that God is savior. Here doing is knowing and knowing is doing. This inseparable symbiosis goes to the heart of Passion Sunday.

The Response: *Psalm 31:9-16*

Living on God's Time

Setting. As another psalm of suffering, Psalm 31:9-16 builds on Isaiah 50:4-9*a*, because it explores the interior reflections of the psalmist during the time of suffering in a way that the suffering servant song did not. Although the suffering of the servant in Isaiah 50:4-9*a* was intense, the point of view of the passage was focused on God and God's reliability during times of suffering. Because of this focus we were never allowed to separate the servant's suffering from God's presence and salvation. Because of this, Isaiah 50:4-9*a* is probably best categorized as a song of confidence. Psalm 31:9-16 takes us further away from the security of God's salvation by exploring the experience of suffering itself. By taking us inside the experience of the suffering psalmist (especially in vv. 11-13) Psalm 31:9-16 becomes a true lament, where confessing the salvation of God is not enough. God must be called upon directly for salvation.

Structure. The psalm for this Sunday is only a fraction of Psalm 31. Most scholars would divide the psalm between vv. 1-8 and 9-24. There is debate, however, on how these two parts are meant to interrelate. Each section appears to be an independent lament. Are they separate psalms that have been brought together? Are they parallel psalms that describe the same experience with increasing intensity? In addition to these larger questions of structure, we should note that a more natural break in the psalm would have been vv. 9-18, since vv. 19-24 is a song of praise that concludes the previous laments (vv. 1-8, 9-18). This discussion of the larger context of Psalm 31 suggests that vv. 9-16 can function well as a unit, even though the call for salvation actually extends through vv. 17-18. Psalm 31:9-16 can be separated into three parts: a call for salvation in vv. 9-10, a description of the psalmist's situation in vv. 11-13, and a confession of, along with a renewed call for, God's salvation in vv. 15-16.

Significance. The structure of Psalm 31:9-16 provides an interesting parallel to the suffering servant song of Isaiah 50:4-9a, since it separates into three parts that show roughly the same movement: from a focus on God, to the experience of the psalmist/suffering servant, and then back to God. As noted above, however, the movement of Psalm 31:9-16 takes us much more deeply through the introspection of the psalmist, which makes this psalm more of a lament than a song of confidence. Although God is the object of the psalm, and, indeed, looms large beneath the surface in every verse, it is the experience of the psalmist, who is presently at a great distance from God's salvation, that takes up most of the imagery. The opening call for salvation in vv. 9-10 ("Be gracious to me, O LORD") gives way immediately to a physical description of the psalmist. Not only are his eyes dissolving (Hebrew, *'ss;* RSV, "wasted") from grief, but his very bones are also dissolving.

Verses 11-13 move us from a physical to a social description of the psalmist. Here we learn that this person radiates dread (Hebrew, *herpa;* NRSV, "the scorn of") to both friends and enemies (v. 11). She is the walking dead (v. 12). This is not idealized suffering. In fact there is no confidence here at all—nothing to grab on to because terror is on every side (v. 13). Up to this point Psalm 31 has described the agony of social alienation and physical breakdown from personal threat. Yet it is here that life itself is also clearly seen for what it is: We all live on God's time (v. 15). This revelation brings the psalmist outside of herself and back to God with a confession of trust along with a renewed call for salvation in vv. 14-16. In reading this psalm and in identifying with the psalmist, we move through the dark pit and dread of Passion Sunday.

New Testament Texts

Both texts are concerned with the Passion and death of Jesus. The brief liturgical piece in Philippians 2 speaks of the "mind" of Christ, indicating the selfless, sacrificial obedience that brought Christ to his death on the cross. Mark offers no such summary, but rather the story of Jesus' final hours of suffering and death, though the telling of the story contains sufficient details and commentary from the evangelist to direct our reflection on Mark's particular view of the Passion.

The Epistle: *Philippians 2:5-11*

Having the Mind of Christ

Setting. The Philippian congregation was the first European church founded by Paul, and it was one with which he maintained a very positive relationship. He was in prison at the time he penned this letter; and he seems to have written for several reasons: (1) to thank the Philippians for their support, physical and spiritual; (2) to discuss Epaphroditus' visit to him in behalf of the Philippians; and (3) to address difficulties and potential problems in the life of the church. Paul spends time early in the body of the letter exhorting the Philippians to unity, beginning at 1:27. In the course of that admonition he holds Christ himself up in a formal fashion as the model and source of Christian harmony.

Structure. Since the late 1920s innumerable scholars have studied Philippians 2:(5)6-11, attempting both to demonstrate that this portion of Philippians is a "Christ-hymn" from the life of the early Church and to determine the hymn's structure, origin, authorship, and theology. At the heart of debate about structure is whether the "hymn" is concerned with celebrating two movements (Christ's humble emptying into human form and Christ's exaltation to heavenly Lordship) or three states (preexistence/human life/Resurrection-exaltation). While these issues are still studied and debated, interpreters are moving toward a middle ground that recognizes the importance of all the elements of both schemes. Whatever the analysis, however, v. 5 is regarded as prose, leading up to the hymn; and vv. 6-11 are seen as the "hymn" per se.

Significance. We can preach much about the range and force of the theological and christological statements contained in this text. Five major thoughts are articulated:

First, the remarks about Jesus Christ's being in the form of God is a metaphorical expression of the conviction of his preexistence. With

77

notable exceptions, few interpreters read the line otherwise. Here, in one of the earliest preserved documents of Christianity is the confession of Christ's preexistence. Often historians assume that belief in preexistence came later in the development of Christian doctrine, but Philippians is testimony to the contrary. Equally remarkable is that Paul, the former Jew, includes and approves such a belief, for there is no evidence that Paul had abandoned Jewish monotheism to make this statement.

Second, Christ's earthly existence is declared using the metaphor of slavery. What does it mean to say that Christ took the form of a slave? The metaphor points to his humble obedience to the will of God and to his faithful service to his fellow human beings as he did God's will.

Third, we hear of Christ's death. The mention of the cross in connection with the death points to the degree of humiliation Christ suffered in order to be faithful to God and humankind. His service was costly. He did not live to a ripe old age and enjoy the fruits of his happy life of service. Indirectly Paul is telling the Philippians (and us) that the Lord died in order to be obedient and faithful—thus, what can disciples expect?

Fourth, Christ's exaltation-resurrection is declared. The phrase, "wherefore also God," introduces this element of the confession. Clearly Christ's being raised and his subsequent exalted status are God's work. Notice, too, that the language ("wherefore") reaches back and relates God's action to Christ's own emptying and self-sacrifice.

Fifth, we learn of Christ's cosmic rule. His self-giving unto death, which issued in God's exalting him, makes him the ruler of the cosmos. The phrases describing the "knees" indicates that all the denizens of heaven, earth, and hell will acknowledge Christ's rule. And the point of that rule is given with the words, "unto the glory of God the Father."

The Gospel: Mark 14:1–15:47

The Son of God Dies for Many

Setting. Mark's whole Gospel is a deliberate effort to define the title, "Son of God." He instructs readers of the Gospel on the meaning of this title by playing it off against another, ''Son of Man'' (see Daniel 7:13). Through the course of the Gospel, prior to Jesus' death on the cross, only supernatural forces—God and the demons—actually recognize that Jesus is the Son of God. To all others Jesus presents himself, referring to himself steadily, as the Son of Man (he alone refers to himself with this title). We come to comprehend who Jesus Christ is as the Son of God only when we follow him through this Gospel as the Son of Man. Who then is the Son of Man? From a reading of the Gospel we can say that Jesus, the Son of Man, is the one who does God's will and God's work in battling the forces of evil for the salvation of humankind. Above all, we learn who Jesus, the Son of Man, is in the course of the Passion narrative when we see him as the one who dies on the cross, giving his life in behalf of humanity for humanity's salvation.

Thus, Jesus, the Son of God, is God's selfless servant who gives himself to save others! He makes provision for the salvation of humanity. He reveals with utter clarity the depth of God's love and the essential, selfless, serving nature of God. And he shows human beings the manner of life to which God calls us all.

Structure. The Passion narrative comprises several distinct scenes that may be viewed in either large or small pieces. Since the lesson presents the whole account, our focus here will be to sketch the general structure of the narrative. Crucial preliminary events are recorded in 14:1-25 (the plot against Jesus, the anointing at Bethany, Judas's collusion with the authorities, and the Passover meal with the institution of the Lord's Supper). Then, in 14:26-52 the scene shifts to the Mount of Olives where Jesus foretells Peter's denial, engages in agonizing prayer, and is arrested. Next, 14:53-72 tells of Jesus' trial before the Council and of Peter's denials. The Roman trial (the delivery by the Council, the inquisition by Pilate, the sentencing of Jesus, and the mockery by the soldiers) is recounted in 15:1-20. Finally 15:21-47 narrates the crucifixion, death, and burial of Jesus.

Significance. Matthew, Mark, and Luke are quite comparable in their manner of narrating the Passion of Jesus, but each brings a distinct perspective to the storytelling that serves as a vehicle for explicating the theological significance of the events. Mark's account communicates several crucial themes related to the death of Jesus.

First, Jesus' death is revelatory. In his willingness to go even to a brutal death on the cross, Jesus embodies the will of God, thus demonstrating the character of suffering love, of power in weakness that is the true character of God. The subsequent observations suggest other ways in which the death is also revelatory.

Second, Jesus' death is expiatory. The word, *expiation,* occurs in Paul's writing (see Romans 3:25), not in Mark's Gospel; but the idea implicit in Mark's narrative is that of expiation through Jesus' death. Expiation is an act that deals with human sin in such a way that the sin itself is put to an end. As Jesus says in Mark 10:45, he came "to give his life as a ransom for many."

Third, Jesus' death is vicarious. As Jesus declares in 14:24 in reference to the cup at the Last Supper, "This is my blood of the covenant, which is poured out for many." His death is said to be in behalf of others. This interpretation does not, however, necessarily lead to the notion of substitutionary penal atonement, where Jesus took upon himself our otherwise rightful punishment. Indeed, such an interpretation flies in the face of the notion of expiation, so that whatever the death of Jesus means, Mark's Gospel casts it as Jesus' act in God's behalf for the sake of humankind, not Jesus' act in our behalf for the sake of God's vengeance.

Fourth, Jesus' death is a victory. Throughout the Gospel we have seen Jesus doing battle in God's behalf against all Satan's forces. Now through death on the cross we find that Jesus, who appears to be defeated by the forces of evil, has invaded the most remote and hopeless corner of Satan's empire, the dark corner of death. In his promise to the disciples (14:28) and through the declaration of his Resurrection (16:6) we find that he has emerged from the conflict having broken Satan's grasp—thus revealing the saving power of God.

Fifth, the death of Jesus means freedom for humankind. Repeatedly in the course of his ministry Jesus acted to liberate humanity from the damning grasp of evil. We see this liberation effected in healings, in exorcisms, in controversy pronouncements, and through teaching. All forms of satanic oppression and all the artificial confinements of human tradition are confronted and defeated so that humans are called to freedom in God's love.

In the Gospel according to Mark, the Passion of Jesus Christ is the story of what God has done for the benefit of humankind. We learn who God is through the saving work of Jesus, God's Son; and we learn who we are called to be as disciples of Jesus Christ, freed from the power of evil and for obedience to God's saving will.

Passion Sunday: The Celebration

For suggestions about the Passion Sunday liturgy, see the above commentary on Holy Week.

The hymn, "All Praise to Thee, for Thou, O King Divine," is a paraphrase of today's epistle, so where there is a concern about the length of the service, it may serve as a hymn or anthem connecting the Old Testament lesson to the reading of the Passion.

It may be a bit overwhelming for the preacher to decide how to preach or what to preach about on this day when faced with such a marvelous array of scripture from which to choose. If the reading of the Passion narrative has been well done, the preacher may feel it anticlimactic to say anything at all! Clearly, the sermon should be focused and to the point, rather than attempting to deal with every aspect of the Passion story in one presentation. One approach is to use the epistle as the hermeneutical key to presenting the theology of the Passion according to whichever Gospel narrative is read. For example, Mark not only records the cry of dereliction, "My God, my God, why have you forsaken me," but he also describes the death of Jesus in the starkest possible terms, he "breathed his last." Here we see dramatically portrayed that self-emptying of which Paul speaks in the epistle lesson as the last drop of life drains from the man on the cross.

Although the primary emphasis of the day is on the Passion rather than the triumphal entry, it might be helpful in congregations where this liturgical approach is new to help them see how the entry is a part of the Passion sequence and introduces us to what is to follow throughout Holy Week. The events of Passion Week are punctuated by scenes of the Temple in Jerusalem. On Sunday Jesus visits the Temple and then returns on Monday to drive out the merchants. He reminds the onlookers that "My house shall be called a house of prayer for all the nations.'' Later in the week he prophesies the destruction of the Temple. And finally, in the account of Jesus' death, Mark quickly shifts the camera from Jesus' last breath to record the rending of the curtain in the Temple, which separated the Holy of Holies—which only the High Priest could enter, and he only once a year—from the rest of the Temple. Jesus' expiatory sacrifice (see exegetical comment above) is understood to be a universal one.

> The veil is rent; in Christ alone
> the living way to heaven is seen;
> the middle wall is broken down,
> and all mankind [the world] may enter in.
> —Charles Wesley

Good Friday

Old Testament Texts

Isaiah 52:13–53:12 is one of the servant songs. Psalm 22 begins as a lament and moves to a hymn of thanksgiving.

The Lesson: *Isaiah 52:13–53:12*

Atonement

Setting. Isaiah 52:13–53:12 is the last of the four servant songs. There has been a progression in the four servants songs, which comes full circle with Isaiah 52:13–53:12. The first poem consisted of a divine announcement concerning the choice of the servant (42:1-4), and the final poem returns to a divine announcement, this time concerning the success of the servant's mission. In neither of these poems does the servant acquire a voice, and this contrasts to the middle two poems (49:1-9 and 50:4-9*a*), where the voice of the servant dominates. The central focus for interpretation and for preaching is to determine what has been the success of the servants' mission.

Structure. A central insight for structuring the poem is to determine the different speakers. Two voices share the poem. Divine announcement opens (52:13-15) and closes (53:11*b*-12) the poem, and these units may, in fact, be one continuous poem now separated. Note the references to the servant in these two sections with the first common singular pronominal suffix ("my servant") in 52:13 and 52:11*b*. Between the two divine announcements a different voice emerges, which is a communal confession about the servant. Note the third common plural pronoun (*we*) and the acknowledgment that God has revealed something through the servant in 53:1. The last servant song, therefore, consists of commentary on the mission of the servant, both by God and by the people of God. The structure suggests that the central focus for interpretation noted above should be divided into two parts: between the assessment of the servant's mission by God and by the community of faith.

Significance. The central point in the divine speeches (52:13-15 and 53:11b-12) is stated in the opening verse: The servant will be exalted (52:13). The remainder of the divine speeches shows how the exaltation of the servant is a surprising reversal on two (related) levels with regard to the appearance of the servant and his power. First, the appearance of the servant in 52:14-15. The imagery in v. 14 suggests that the servant is hideous, so much so that people are repelled by the freak. One is reminded here of the play *Elephant Man,* where the main character was so deformed that he wore a sheet over his head to keep from terrifying people. Verse 15 describes an equally strong reaction to the servant (''so he will startle many nations''). The syntax of the two verses, however, suggests that this reaction is not prompted by the disfigured appearance of the servant, but by his mission, which clashes with his looks.

Second, the mission of the servant in 53:11b-12. Verse 11b underscores how the freak is in fact righteous and, even more, how he is able to transmit this quality to others. Verse 12 builds on the insight of v. 11b by describing how such a transmission of righteousness is possible. To paraphrase the text, we could say that the servant is like a sponge with the ability to absorb the transgression of others into himself. One suspects that the emphasis on freakish disfigurement in the opening speech (52:12-15) is meant to be a metaphor for the action of atonement that is described in the closing speech (54:11b-12). It is because the servant has absorbed the transgressions of the people of God that he appears the freak. In other words, his appearance is a mirror of the true state of a humanity prior to atonement.

The speeches by the people of God presuppose the divine revelation concerning the mission of the servant. Thus 53:1-11a must be read as confession mixed with surprise. This section separates into three parts. It opens with a statement of surprise in v. 1, followed by two speeches (vv. 2-6 and 7-11a), which share the same structure as the two divine speeches by also contrasting appearance (vv. 2-3 and 7-9) with the real mission of the servant (vv. 4-6 and 10-11a). In the first speech (vv. 2-6) the congregation connects the freakish appearance of the servant (vv. 2-3) with the insight that the disfigurement was in fact due to their guilt, here conceived as disease (vv. 4-6). In the second speech (vv. 7-11a) the congregation takes the next step and realizes that the death of the servant (vv. 7-9) was not simply unjust oppression, but in fact a guilt offering (Hebrew, 'asam) for them (vv. 10-11a).

Interpretation up to this point has been traditional-historical. This means that the two divine speeches in 52:12-15 and 53:11b-12 could function independently from the speeches of the congregation in 52:1-11b, and that is how we have interpreted them. But that is not how they function in the present form of the text, and this raises a question of how the two different voices interrelate in the final servant song.

We have recognized that Isaiah 52:13–53:12 is a message about atonement. The interrelationship of the two voices in the present form of the text provides insight into atonement and how it functions. First, atonement is about human corruption conceived as disease. Such an understanding of sin goes far beyond human motive (ethics) in order to focus on the condition of humanity. Hence the imagery of disease that is used in 53:4, where sin is like a facial cancer—it disfigures and kills indiscriminately.

Second, the disfigurement and death of the servant, as an act of atonement, is not obvious. In fact, this deadly experience appears to be the opposite of atonement—punishment by God (53:4). Because of this paradox between appearance and reality, the disfigurement and death of the servant functions only as a potential antidote (or compensation) to the disease of sin.

Third, effective atonement requires that the atoned one participate in the event and realize that the action is taking place. This insight is made through the present structure of the text. Note that the description of the servant's death as a guilt offering (Hebrew, 'asam) is stated by the congregation in 53:10 and not by God. It is the congregation that must see beyond the appearance of the servant to his divine mission, and only then is their confession followed by the closing divine speech in 53:11b-12, which functions not as new revelation about the servant but as a confirmation of the insight by the congregation.

We Christians understandably have a strong tendency to read this servant song christologically with reference to the one-time event of Jesus' Passion in the historical past. Atonement is the most powerful gift that God offers humanity, but it can never be conceived of solely as a once-and-for-all event, because its effectiveness requires that those being relieved of guilt enter into the event and understand what is happening. Thus, atonement must also be conceived of as a present and repeatable power in the ongoing life of the worshiping community.

The Response: *Psalm 22*

An Archetype for the Passion

Setting. Psalm 22 is quoted frequently throughout the New Testament Passion narratives (Matthew 27:35, 39, 43, 46; Mark 15:29, 34; John 19:23-24, 28). The many quotations underscore the influential role that this psalm played in the actual formation of the Passion story.

Structure. Psalm 22 separates into two clearly divided units. Verses 1-21 is a lament in which themes of abandonment by God are probed. The turning point is stated in v. 21b with the words, ''From the horns of the wild oxen you have rescued me.'' Verses 22-31 then change direction and take on the language of praise and thanksgiving in light of the divine rescue noted in v. 21b.

Significance. Two points are noteworthy for using Psalm 22 on Good Friday. First, the psalm is archetypal, for it provides the full range of liturgical language, from despair to thanksgiving. Because of this full range of expression, one can see how this psalm would have influenced the early church in its interpretation of the Passion of Jesus. Second, the psalm is communal in its orientation. This conclusion appears to be contradicted by the lonely declaration of God-forsaken-ness in the opening verse. The psalmist is certainly facing the threat of death alone in vv. 1-2, but the imagery of community enters into the psalm immediately in vv. 3-5 and remains a central part. Past tradition looms large in vv. 3-5 as a source of hope when the psalmist laments her imminent death. Then when salvation breaks into the present, the psalmist turns in praise to the congregation in vv. 22 and 25. Finally, either the psalmist or the entire congregation shifts their focus to the future community in vv. 30-31 by noting how this present incident of salvation will become part of tradition, with the result that a future sufferer will be able to look back upon it for encouragement at a time of lament just as the singer of Psalm 22 did in vv. 3-5. Psalm 22 is certainly an archetypal experience, but the archetype is less about an idealized individual than it is about an idealized community.

New Testament Texts

The lessons focus our attention on the death of Jesus. The passage from Hebrews is a meditation on the "sacrifice" of Christ and the significance of its results. The text from the Fourth Gospel narrates the trial and death of Jesus. Hebrews is keenly interested in making application of the christological message to the living of Christian life, but John's text is more interested in focusing on God's accomplishments through Jesus and how Jesus moved magisterially through the course of his Passion, all the while in charge of the events.

The Epistle: *Hebrews 10:16-25*

Christ's Sacrifice and Our Life of Faith

Setting. Some commentators regard the verses of this lesson as the closing segment of a larger section treating the meaning of Christ's great sacrifice and its application to Christian life (8:1–10:25). Other interpreters contend that the verses are from both the ending of one section on Christ's death (8:1–10:18) and the beginning of another that deals with the new and living way of faith for believers (10:19–12:29). Whichever understanding one holds, it is the case that the text is located at or near a pivot in the epistle. Thus, the verses of the lesson present reflection upon both Christ's death and the meaning of that death as the basis of the new life of Christians.

Structure. There are two broad movements in the lesson. First, vv. 16-18 speak of the new covenant, which is the fulfillment of God's promises. This covenant is presented as a divinely accomplished reality, and it is interpreted to mean that the old sacrificial system has been superseded and is, therefore, irrelevant. Second, vv. 19-25 seek to apply the teaching about the new covenant to the lives of the believers, saying that through the sacrifice of Jesus believers have access to holy space wherein their lives are purified and their relationships are redefined. Covenant freedom, Christ's sacrifice, and a new context and way of life are the themes of this lesson.

Significance. The two parts of the lesson correlate the accomplishments of God through Jesus Christ with the new manner of living of believers, basing the latter on the former and urging persons of faith to live up to what God has done for them. God is the covenant-maker according to our lesson. Covenant is a pact, a compact, a mutually restricting and mutually beneficial agreement that forms the basis of a relationship between two parties. Remarkably, however, in relation to the new covenant of which our lesson speaks, God promised this covenant, God acted to effect this covenant, and humans basically derive benefits from what God has done, doing little to nothing themselves to establish this covenant! Good news, indeed!

The verses prior to this lesson reflect on Christ's sacrifice (death) and his preeminent priesthood (resurrection-exaltation?). Hebrews uses the quotation from Jeremiah in vv. 16-17 to interpret the work of God in Christ as God's establishment of a new covenant. As the old covenant had sacrifices and priests, the new covenant has one sacrifice and one priest, the same Jesus Christ. Hebrews declares that the old covenant functioned externally in relation to its participants, but now we learn that one of the blessings of the new covenant is that God has worked through Jesus Christ to make the new covenant an internal affair, written on human hearts and, thus, transforming human lives. We do not merely live up to the conditions of the covenant of Christ, rather, because of its radical internal character, we live out of its powerful standards. All this means a newly given freedom for us as participants in the new covenant. Through Christ, God has established a new basis of relating to humans that frees us through absolute forgiveness. God's action in Christ frees us from the past to live in the freedom of God's previously promised and now fulfilled present and future.

Verses 19-25 issue a call to commitment by extending the metaphor of priestly sacrifice from the prior section(s). Now, Hebrews expounds the meaning of Christian life through a since-this-then-that argument. To paraphrase, "Since because of the work of Christ we have a new relationship to God, then let us live in faith, let us live in hope, and let us live in a new relationship with one another." Christian freedom means a new life of confidence in God, a new life of expectation that God will continue in an even greater way the work already begun, and a new selfless pattern of community life where we worship together and give mutual support to one another for the edification of the community of faith. With faith and hope in God, yielding a life of confidence and expectation, we are called together into a corporate life of celebration and realization of God's purposes.

The Gospel: *John 18:1–19:42*

The Striking Story of Christ's Glory

Setting. Having recognized the arrival of his hour—namely, the time of his Passion, death, resurrection, and exaltation in chapter 12—Jesus concluded his public ministry. (Readers may refer to the comments on the Gospel lesson for the Fifth Sunday in Lent for further information about the arrival of the "hour.") Commentators frequently refer to the second part of the Fourth Gospel (13:1–20:31) as "the book of glory," indicating that the story of Jesus' hour is the story of his glorification in fulfilling God's purposes. Chapter 13 recounts Jesus' last meal with his disciples. Chapters 14–17 record Jesus' last discourse and his prayers for his disciples and all believers. Chapters 18–19 tell the story of Jesus' Passion, narrating the events of the Passion from the garden to the grave.

Structure. The Passion narrative in the gospel according to John is a unified, but elaborate, structure. The story is highly dramatic, and its structure matches the character of the account. We find a brief scene in the garden (18:1-12) followed by the blended scenes of Jesus before Annas (18:13-14, 19-24) and Peter in the courtyard of the high priest (18:15-18, 25-27). This leads to the trial before Pilate (18:28–19:16), which scholars regularly suggest unfolds in a series of seven scenes (18:28-32; 18:33-38*a*; 18:38*b*-40; 19:1-3; 19:4-8; 19:9-12*a*; and 19:12*b*-16). The story of Jesus being put to death is told in 19:17-37, followed by the account of the burial (19:38-42). The preacher confronts an embarrassment of riches in this narrative, in the stories, in the lines spoken, and in the exchanges between Jesus and the other characters. The pageantry of this passage can be well communicated through an organized, multivoice reading of the text. Such a dramatic liturgical presentation takes careful planning and practice, but it is a rewarding experience in worship to present such a production.

Significance. The length of this lesson makes detailed exposition of its significance impossible, so the following comments focus on the text as a whole.

The Passion of Jesus in John's Gospel is the hour of his glory. This time comes as the climax and realization of Jesus' entire mission. John's portrait of Jesus emphasizes his regal demeanor as he moves through the various moments of the story. He is in the story, but strikingly John presents him as all the while above the story. It is by his own free will that he submits to unjust and ignoble treatment from his adversaries, and it is through these horrible events that he returns to his heavenly Father. From that exalted position he promises and later imparts the gift of the Spirit. From one point of view the death of Jesus brings his life to its purposeful ending, but from another, higher perspective, the events of the Passion are the new beginning of the greater chapter of Christ's story. One reading John's account should never take lightly the brutal turns and twists of the events, but one should never be overwhelmed by the negative elements, for the character of Christ is steadfastness and determination dominates the narrative.

As Jesus strides boldly through the course of the Passion, he acts as Lord over all others in the story. Through what he accomplishes in the Passion, Jesus Christ effects a cosmic judgment that separates light from darkness. Thus, both redemption and condemnation are accomplished through his death. Yet as the one "lifted up"—both on the cross and through resurrection—Christ ultimately brings healing as he provokes repentance as the exalted icon of the very love of God. From the crucified Jesus new life streams into the world as God effects cleansing and purification from sinfulness for the sake of God's children.

John's account never cracks open the codes of salvation in this account of Jesus' Passion. Rather, Jesus' own confidence calls the believer to embrace the good news of saving love without the necessity of a mechanical explanation of how the mystery of God's work through Jesus Christ operates. The story presents Jesus as the Paschal Lamb provided by God for the benefit of humanity. Yet, John's account presents Jesus Christ and the benefits of his Passion without seeking to explain the mystery of grace. Grace is shown and declared. God's grace in Jesus Christ is presented with the expectation that an encounter with that grace will draw the children of God from darkness to light by the saving power of God present in Jesus Christ, crucified and raised. This story is the account of God's mystery of salvation, accomplished in Jesus Christ. It is told, above all, to draw humans into the transforming experience of God's grace.

Good Friday: The Celebration

It should be evident from the choice of lessons in the lectionary that the liturgical setting is intended to be a service of the word much like that of the Lord's Day. For congregations that meet for an hour or so in the afternoon or in the evening, this presents no problem. For congregations that are accustomed to the *tre ore*, the three-hour service, usually with a series of meditations on the words from the cross, some new considerations will arise. Few persons attend the entire three-hour service, and in the present culture fewer persons have an opportunity to be in church at all at noon on Good Friday. Those who "drop in" experience an incomplete liturgical event with little sense of how the beginning is connected to the end, if it is at all. The stringing together of the seven statements, or "words" of Jesus from the cross seeks to effect a harmonization of the Gospels, which is exegetically questionable.

The worship committee may wish to determine when the largest number of the congregation might conveniently gather on Good Friday—at noon, sometime between noon and three, or in the evening—and schedule the main service of the day at that time. If there are those who wish to observe the three hours' devotion in its entirety, then perhaps the first two hours might be devoted to extended times of profound silence punctuated by special music and acts of worship. A full half-hour of silence should then precede the community liturgy at 2:00 P.M.

We emphasize once again on Good Friday that our Christian community knows what it is celebrating; we are not re-enacting it, for to do so is to manipulate the congregation. A tension can be maintained responsibly between the grief we experience over the tragedy of the Crucifixion and the joy of the Resurrection about which we already know. We do not enter into the mystery of Good Friday pretending that Easter has not happened. It is, after all, God's Friday, not the powers of death, so even here the note of triumph is to be sounded, as in such hymns as "In the Cross of Christ I Glory" (to be found in many hymnals), "Sing, My Tongue, the Glorious Battle" (Episcopal 165-66; United Methodist 296), "The Royal Banners Forward Go" (Episcopal 162; Lutheran 124-25), "Sunset to Sunrise" (Episcopal 163; UCC 132), "We Sing the Praise of Him Who Died" (Episcopal 471; Ms. Syn. Lutheran 118), and "My Song Is Love Unknown" (Episcopal 458; Mennonite 172; UCC 74).

A recent significant change in liturgical practice is the use of dark red (passion red) rather than black as the color of the day. The use of black as a negative color has serious implications in a society where racism is a constant concern and threat, because it subliminally communicates a message that the white of Easter is good and the black of Good Friday is bad. Passion red calls to mind the shed blood of Christ who died for all of us who were made by God of one blood (Acts 17:26). The red may be used to drape the cross on the altar or the holy table and for the vestments of the clergy, but no other adornment should be used; and there should not be other crosses in the liturgical environment competing for attention. The chancel should be quite bare.

Roman Catholics and Episcopalians have made provision in their new liturgies for the distribution of communion on Good Friday from the elements consecrated the day before. The earlier tradition was that of no celebration of the Eucharist and no Communion after the

Maundy Thursday service until the first service of Easter (usually the Vigil). The value of the older tradition is that it keeps a steady movement towards the climactic moment of the Easter eucharist rather than stopping to "feast" on a fast day. Excellent liturgical resources and model orders of worship for Good Friday may be found in the *New Handbook of the Christian Year*.

EASTER: CREATION'S EIGHTH DAY

Although Easter is the central, formative event in the Christian revelation, and although it is the day of the largest attendance of the faithful at church, it frequently has an anticlimactic character after all of the emphasis put into Lent. Easter Day, the day towards which the Lenten solemnity has been directed, ends up marking both the high point in the year's attendance and the beginning of the downward spiral towards the summer low point.

This may be because Easter is finally mystery, a wonderfully overwhelming mystery, and the human creature cannot for long bear what it cannot understand. We are familiar with the miracle of birth, and so we concur with the sentiment that Christmas should be kept all the year long. I have seen men and women leave the church weeping after the solemn stripping of the altar on Maundy Thursday, because we know what it is to have rejoicing turned into mourning, to surrender the brightness of life to the shadow of death. Maybe that is why Easter is so unbearable: It dares to proclaim a reality opposed to that which we experience in the natural realm. We hear no one suggesting that we keep Easter all the year long, even though the observance of the Lord's Day every seven days intends precisely that!

The Christian year and lectionary seek to make us aware that Easter is more than one day in the year and to restore the historic observance of the Great Fifty Days, the time from Easter Day through the Day of Pentecost. No longer do we speak of Sundays "after Easter," but "of Easter," reminding us that the celebration is an ongoing event in the Church's life of prayer and proclamation. Pentecost is not the first day of a new season; it is the last day of the Easter festival, uniting the events of the Resurrection and the empowerment of the Church. The Great Fifty Days are observed as a unity because they are presented that way in the Lukan chronology. In John's Gospel, the risen Lord breathes the Holy Spirit upon the apostles on the evening of Easter Day. The Christian year achieves a kind of liturgical harmonization of the Gospels by placing the Day of Pentecost in the evening of the season. The observance of sacred time thus helps teach us that the Resurrection, the Ascension, and the gift of the Spirit are mutually dependent events participating in the same theological reality. Each presupposes the others.

It has not been unknown in the history of Christian preaching for the Easter proclamation to lose its radical character and for the theological center to be ignored in the interest of making the day more palatable to modern sensibilities. This began early in the English-speaking world, since the day was called "Easter," after the pagan goddess of spring, rather than some form of the word *Pasch,* which was the practice in the Romance languages. Pagan symbolism has frequently dominated the observance and turned it into a kind of vernal rite, complete with the fertility images of eggs and rabbits. Spring symbolism has ended up as the content of the Easter message, and Resurrection is reduced to a biological necessity, a regeneration of the earth, while we rejoice in our hymns that "Flowers make glee among the hills,/ And set the meadows dancing"! It is salutary for those of us in the northern hemisphere to remember that in half the world Easter occurs in the autumn.

The other way in which the radical proclamation of Easter has often been compromised has been through substituting a platonic doctrine of the immortality of the soul for the biblical concept of resurrection. Eternal life is seen as something we have a "right" to rather than the free gift of God in Jesus Christ. To the degree that we are immortal, it is in relation to what God has done in salvation rather than creation. That salvation is the cause for our Easter proclamation and celebration.

As Lent has dealt with the issue of mortality, beginning with Ash Wednesday, so now Easter celebrates that immortality which is God's gift, the antidote to sin's poison. The Easter Vigil has been restored in the practice of many churches because it presents in a unified fashion

95

the story of sin and salvation in the lessons and applies that story by means of the sign-act of baptism to the life of the individual believer who is made a part of the Body of Christ and is nourished spiritually at the Lord's Table. Pastors and worship committees unfamiliar with the Vigil should consult the *New Handbook of the Christian Year* to find a copy of the service and helpful commentary about it.

Many preachers and worship leaders are dismayed when first they look at the list of lessons for the Vigil and the length of the service. At this point of fatigue we need to remember that the liturgy was made for them and not they for the liturgy. Without endorsing some kind of liturgical minimalism, it is possible to ask what is reasonable for a congregation unfamiliar with this particular tradition and to ask what is most important within this service.

Historically, the Vigil was the time for the baptism of those who had received instruction and their participation for the first time in the Lord's Supper. The reading of the history of salvation lasted through the night, leading to the baptism, the illumination, of the converts as the sun began to rise and they were buried and raised with Christ in baptism. This intricate interweaving of story and song, light and darkness, water and oil, touching and being touched, bread and wine, is eloquent testimony to the Church's understanding of the liturgy as a multimedia event!

For churches locked into an hour time frame, it is obvious that the Vigil in its fullness will have difficulty gaining acceptance. Pastors might wish to think of spreading the components of the Vigil out over a period of time. This maintains the sequence of events in their integrity, and as they move through the Sundays of Easter they help the congregation focus on the Paschal mystery throughout the season.

The four sections of the Vigil (light, Word, water, Eucharist) may be divided among the first three Sundays of Easter by doing the service of light as part of the traditional sunrise service, the service of the Word as the "regular service" on Easter Day, the administration of baptism on the Second Sunday of Easter where the epistle reading from I John with its emphasis on cleansing from sin will be appropriate, and the Lord's Supper on the Third Sunday of Easter when the Gospel reading tells of the risen Christ eating with the apostles. The Fourth through the Seventh Sundays of Easter may then be devoted to what has been called "mystagogical catechesis," training in the meaning of these sacred mysteries in which we have participated. Commentary on the lessons of the Vigil will be found in *Year A: Lent/Easter* in this commentary series.

Baptism is central to our celebration of Easter, and Easter is central to our understanding of baptism. The Lord's Day is the eighth day of creation, the day of the new creation brought into being by Christ's victory over death. In a time when baptism is the center of so much theological discussion and controversy, pastors and people might do well to explore and experience the meaning of baptism from a liturgical perspective rather than to argue about meaning in terms of static, academic categories.

This may mean "saving up" baptisms for Easter, so that there will be individuals ready to receive the Easter sacrament. This in itself testifies to an understanding of baptism which mantains that it is not an individualistic rite, but a community one. The baptisms might be spread across the Great Fifty Days. This allows some convenience in timing, but it also emphasizes the meaning of the whole season. More than one baptism should be done at a time whenever possible, however, so as not to lose the communal nature of the event.

The renewal of baptismal vows is a part of many Vigil services, especially if there are no baptisms to be administered, but if there is no Vigil, as with other components mentioned above, it may find an independent place during one of the Sunday services of the season. The main service of Easter Day itself is preferable, since the renewal service can be a vivid reminder of what brings everyone, the regulars and the one-timers, together in the Christian family. A brief form of baptismal renewal may be used for the rest of the Sundays of Easter at the beginning of the service as part of the entrance rite and in place of the confession of sin, as follows:

> Alleluia! Christ is risen.
> The Lord is risen indeed. **Alleluia!**
> Let us pray.
> God of the Covenants,
> we thank you for this gift of water
> which gives fruitfulness to the fields
> and refreshment and cleansing to your creatures.

Water witnessed to your goodness
when you led your people through the sea
and satisfied their thirst from flinty rock.
You consecrated your Son
in the waters of the Jordan,
and through water
you have given us a new birth from above.
May this water remind us of our baptism,
and let us share the joy
of all who have been baptized this Easter.
We ask this in the name of the Risen Christ.
Amen.
Sprinkling water towards the people, the minister says:
Remember your baptism and be thankful.
The service continues with the opening hymn.*

Baptisms are possibly the most ecumenically segregated events in the Christian Church. The sign act that is understood to incorporate us into the catholic Church is most often observed in congregational isolation. Easter can be a time to realize the fullness of the sign by administering baptism in company with other congregations, so that its ecumenical character is realized. This can easily be done when two or more churches celebrate the Easter Vigil together.

*Based on a prayer for the blessing of water in *All God's People: The New Ecumenical Prayer Cycle—Orders of Service,* John Carden, ed. (Geneva: World Council of Churches, 1989), p. 110.

Easter Day

Old Testament Texts

Isaiah 25:6-9 describes a divine banquet on Mount Zion, and Psalm 118:1-2, 14-24 is a song of thanksgiving.

The Lesson: *Isaiah 25:6-9*

A Banquet on Zion

Setting. Isaiah 25:6-9 is best read as an example of apocalyptic theology. A modest understanding of apocalyptic thought is possible by contrasting this form of prophecy with classical prophecy in terms of theology and sociology.

A central feature in classical prophecy is a correspondence between the visions and words of the prophet and the present social system. Even though prophets were frequently critical of either the king or some other aspect of Israelite life, the prophet might always assume that the message could prompt immediate change. Two consequences follow from this presumption about change. (1) Theologically, classical prophets understood God to be involved intimately in both the life of Israel and in the larger events of history. (2) Sociologically, the assumption of classical prophets that an oracle could instantly change behavior calls into question a common perception of prophets as outsiders without real power in the ongoing social life of Israel. Classical prophets had perceived social power, and their criticism could change the policy of the king.

Apocalyptic thought is a complex development whose origin and influence in later Israelite religion are still under study. For our purposes apocalypticism may be characterized by contrasting it to the theology and sociology of classical prophecy. Theologically, apocalyptic literature neither shares the confidence that God is willing to redeem or fix day-to-day problems in the human condition, nor does it assume that God is directing ongoing world events toward an immediate and compromised end. We might say that apocalyptic literature is less optimistic about the degree to which God's salvation can be realized in the present time, and about the purposefulness of history.

This lack of optimism is usually reinforced by the present social context of apocalyptic writers. Unlike classical prophets, these writers were usually in a position where they could not influence the social policy or the beliefs of the larger worshiping community. Apocalypticists, therefore, tended to be outsiders, yet they maintained the faith. In view of this, the theological focus of apocalypticism tends to be on the distant future, where God is perceived as breaking into this present evil world, destroying it, and fashioning a new one in which only the faithful would dwell. The imagery illustrates how apocalypticism is a disjunctive form of faith. It is disjunctive because belief in the salvation of God is maintained even though all of life's experience states that such a faith could not possibly be true. With this as background it is easy to see how the resurrection of Jesus in the early Church was formed in the larger context of apocalyptic literature. Our focus is on an earlier example of apocalyptic writing, Isaiah 25:6-9.

Structure. Isaiah 24–27 is often considered to be a self-contained unit with the book of Isaiah, because a great deal of the imagery within it turns to end-time visions of salvation. Isaiah 25:6-9 fits well into the context of Isaiah 24–27 because it provides an end-time vision of God hosting a banquet on Mount Zion. The text separates into at least two parts. Isaiah 25:6-8 describes the salvation that will take place on Mount Zion. This section has close links to Isaiah 24:21-23 where God's defeat of heavenly and earthly enemies is described, and where the reign of God on Mount Zion is specifically stated. The opening reference to "this mountain" in 25:6 links the two passages even more closely because it is meant to refer back to Mount Zion in 24:23. Isaiah 25:9 begins a new section that continues through v. 12. This section includes a song of thanksgiving in vv. 9-10*a* and a description of the destruction of the Moabites in vv. 10*b*-12. The extension of the song of thanksgiving through v. 10*a* provides a strong reason to expand the lectionary text to include at least the hymn in vv. 9-10*a*.

Significance. Apocalyptic literature is frequently characterized by an extensive use of mythology. The vision of salvation in apocalyptic literature is normally cosmic in scope (usually including a new creation), for which ancient Near Eastern mythology provided a vast reservoir of images. Three features of Isaiah 25:6-9 become clearer when they are viewed in the larger context of ancient Near Eastern mythology.

First, the setting of Mount Zion. Most gods live on mountains. Mount Olympus as the home of Zeus in Greek mythology comes to mind. In closer proximity to Israel, we could mention the Canaanite god, Baal, who lived on Mount Zaphon. The ancients believed that temples provided the channel where God was able to enter our world, and the imagery of elevation associated with moutains was meant to communicate this belief. The Lord is connected with a number of mountains in the Old Testament (Mount Sinai, Mount Moriah, Mount Horeb), but perhaps the most prominent mountain home for God is Mount Zion. Mount Zion has a specific geographical location in Jerusalem, where it referred to the Temple, but the symbol goes beyond reference to the Temple to envisage a whole new world in which God is present. An early example of the relationship between Temple and world occurs in Psalm 48:1 where the psalmist moves easily between specific geography and mythological or cosmological imagery in referring to Zion. Note how at one minute Zion is in "the city" where the Temple is located, and, then, how it is located in "the far north," which in Hebrew is the word *Zaphon*, Baal's mountain home. The reference to "the far north" goes beyond geography in order to envision a qualitatively different world, in which God is present. Vestiges of this kind of use of geography carry over in modern life in our reference to Santa Claus, who, we state confidently, also lives in the far north. If you have a small child, who wants to get in the car and drive north to see Santa, then you know firsthand how reference to geography can become a symbol about a qualitatively different kind of world. This is also true of Zion. Although it described a specific mountain in Jerusalem, it also encompassed a vision of a new world order. We might summarize our discussion in the following way: mountains symbolize temples, because the latter were confessed to be the point where heaven and earth meet, with the result that God could be present with the worshiping community. Modern church steeples symbolize the same belief. The setting of the mountain is essential for interpreting Isaiah 25:6-9.

Second, the content of the vision. Two things happen in this vision: (1) God hosts a banquet on Mount Zion, and (2) God defeats death. Both of these events are firmly rooted in Canaanite mythology, where Baal hosts a banquet for the gods on his holy mountain, Zaphon, after he constructs his temple. In the larger structure of Canaanite mythology, Baal's banquet must be interpreted as his momentary defeat of death, symbolized as the god, Mot, who will later defeat Baal in the cyclical combat between life and death (fertility and infertility) that is central to Canaanite religion. The writer of Isaiah 25:6-9 has taken over these images from Canaanite mythology to make a theological statement about the power of God to recreate and to save. If we take seriously the theological and social context of apocalyptic literature outlined above, then we must recognize that these powerful images of an end-time salvation are not an affirmation of experience, but a call to faith in spite of experience. This interpretation is supported by the song of thanksgiving in vv. 9-10a. This song is not an affirmation of the experience of the present worshiping community, but is placed in the future time ("It will be said on that day."). The language of the song indicates that the present worshiping community is best characterized as waiting for a salvation that is not yet realized. The result of this future orientation is that the images of salvation in vv. 6-8 provide both hope for tomorrow and a springboard for critically evaluating today.

It is easy to see the roots of much Easter imagery in Isaiah 25:6-9 with regards to the vanquishing of death in the Passion of Jesus and the resultant messianic banquet. These motifs from Isaiah 25:6-9 gain a distinctively Christian cast in New Testament literature because they acquire contemporary significance in light of the mission of Jesus. The danger for Christians is precisely at this point, for resurrection can never be reduced to an affirmation of present experience. Early Christian writers underscored this by locating resurrection within the future orientation of apocalyptic thinking. Easter must incorporate a confession about the future, and thus provide the springboard for critically evaluating our present lives. A central challenge for preaching on Easter is to reintroduce this subversive (or perhaps better, disjunctive) quality to our all-too-comfortable Easter faith. Easter is still more about tomorrow than it is about today. Thus, the very celebration of it carries a challenge of discipleship.

The Response: *Psalm 118:1-2, 14-24*

A Song of Thanksgiving

Setting. The imagery of the gate in v. 19 clearly locates Psalm 118 in the context of the Temple, where the psalm must have functioned in some kind of entrance liturgy (see also Psalm 24). The imagery of a procession of worshipers moving up to the Temple (vv. 14-18), requesting to enter (vv. 19-20), and then thanking God for the right to enter the sanctuary (vv. 21-24) is central to any interpretation.

Structure. Psalm 118 separates into three parts. Verses 1-4 and 22-29 are the voice of a chorus, and they frame an individual song of thanksgiving in vv. 5-21. The lectionary text incorporates aspects of the opening chorus (1-2), the individual song of thanksgiving (vv. 14-21), and the closing chorus (vv. 22-24).

Significance. The psalm provides an important counterpoint to Isaiah 25:6-9. The movement of the processional from outside of the Temple (vv. 14-18), through the gates (vv. 19-21), and into the sanctuary (vv. 22-24) emphasizes the present quality of salvation that was absent from the future perspective of Isaiah 25:6-9. This movement in the psalm—toward a realization of salvation within the worshiping community—was also noticed by New Testament writers, who use it to interpret Jesus as the cornerstone of the Temple (see, for example, Matthew 21:42, Mark 12:10, Luke 20:17).

New Testament Texts

The passage from I Corinthians 15 recalls the essential early Christian teaching about Jesus' death and resurrection. The two grand

Gospel lessons—the lectionary provides for the use of John in Years A, B, and C—tell of the empty tomb, and while there are marked similarities between their stories, the contrast between them is striking. Each author brings a particular perspective to the storytelling and formulates an account with a distinct perspective.

The Epistle: *I Corinthians 15:1-11**

Recalling the Most Basic Matters

Setting. Repeatedly throughout I Corinthians Paul declares a topic and proceeds to reflect upon it for the benefit of the Corinthians. For example, at I Corinthians 1:1 Paul refers to the report he received concerning the quarreling Corinthians and, then, he goes on to address this problem; and at 7:1 Paul mentions "the matters about which [the Corinthians] wrote" before reflecting upon appropriate sexual relations among the members of the church. In 15:1-11, however, Paul launches into the consideration of a problem that he does not name until 15:12—namely, that some of the members of the church in Corinth are denying there is a resurrection of the dead. Paul considered the problem so severe that he relays in 15:1-11 a foundation that he had previously laid in Corinth. Then, Paul works off this foundation in relation to the problem in the remainder of chapter 15.

Structure. Paul introduces his presentation of the basic tradition concerning Christ's death and resurrection in vv. 1-2. Then, in the language of liturgical formulation he presents the fundamental tradition in vv. 3-8. After delivering the tradition anew, in vv. 9-11 Paul applies the "meaning" of the teaching to himself and to the Corinthians. Thus, we find (1) introduction, (2) tradition, and (3) application/interpretation—a logical structure for a logical presentation. We should notice, moreover, that the traditional material in vv. 3-8 is neatly structured: (a) death, (b) burial, (c) Resurrection, and (d) appearances. Herein, the burial confirms the reality of the death as the appearances confirm the reality of the Resurrection; and the crucial

*Acts 10:34-43 is the alternate second reading for Years A, B, C; see Year A, Baptism of the Lord (p. 103) for commentary.

items, death and Resurrection, are both said to have occurred in accordance with the Scriptures.

Significance. This is a rich but difficult passage. Consultation of several good commentaries is crucial. The key to understanding what Paul is up to in these verses is to see that he is concerned with arguing for the reality of the Resurrection. Thus, we should not be surprised that while Paul says Christ's death took place in relation to humanity's sinfulness and in accordance with the Scriptures, he does not attempt to explain what he means. Christ's death and its significance are not Paul's concerns here, and while these issues are themselves crucial, the present passage is perhaps not the one in relation to which the preacher should attempt to ponder the saving significance of Christ's dying.

Instead, let us follow Paul's lead and turn to Christ's Resurrection. Paul declares with illustrated vigor the reality of the Resurrection. The Christ who died and was buried was really raised from the dead. Paul knows this because the raised Jesus appeared to Cephas, to the twelve, to more than 500 disciples at once, to James, to all the apostles, and to Paul himself. Paul illustrates the reality of the Resurrection out of the realm of wishful thinking, fantasy, or hallucination. The exact nature of the appearances is itself not Paul's concern, rather he argues for the reality of the Resurrection through references to the several appearances of the raised Christ.

With the confessional line ''in accordance with the scriptures'' Paul reports the early Christian evaluation of Christ's death and Resurrection. This understanding of the death and Resurrection is the perspective of faith. Inherent in this understanding is the conviction that Christ's death and Resurrection occurred according to the will of God. Paul's teaching about the reality of the Resurrection declares that the power of God that raised Jesus from the dead mysteriously and mercifully made of his death a saving event that dealt with the sinful condition of humanity.

Moreover, the power that raised Jesus also transformed Paul and, Paul says, it was at work transforming the Corinthians as they heard the preaching and believed. As the Resurrection overturns the death of Jesus, it demonstrates the power of God, which transforms Christ's death into salvation as it transforms sinful human lives and saves through faith in Christ's death and Resurrection. The reality of the Resurrection shows the reality of the power of God, which alters reality itself—raising the dead Jesus, altering Paul the zealous persecutor into Paul the energetic apostle, and transforming the Corinthians from being people who were steeped in sin to be people who are being saved.

The Gospel: *John 20:1-18*

Seeing and Believing

Setting. After the Passion narrative (from the garden to the grave—see the comments on the Gospel lesson for Good Friday in this volume) the story of God's work through Jesus Christ pauses briefly as the characters in the story observe the Sabbath. Then, with the Sabbath having created a disjunction in the account, we move to the first day of the week (Sunday) and rejoin the story by following the activities of Mary Magdalene and certain of Jesus' disciples.

Structure. The lesson presents the initial discoveries and reactions of Mary and the disciples followed by the account of Mary's encounter with the risen Lord. The alternating focus is striking. It creates dramatic tension and contrasts faith perspectives. In vv. 1-2 we find Mary seeing but not believing or understanding. Then, in vv. 3-10 we follow Simon Peter and the beloved disciple as they visit the tomb and see (or, don't see!) and believe, although they do not fully understand. Then, in vv. 11-18 Mary encounters the risen Jesus; and while she sees, she initially does not understand, although through this meeting she comes to believe and to understand. One, two, or all of these scenes may serve as the text for preaching. However the text is employed, one should notice the distinct ways in which seeing, believing, and understanding are related to one another.

Significance. The symbolic nature of the events that transpire in the verses of our lesson are highlighted at the outset of the storytelling when John says that Mary Magdalene came to the tomb while it was still dark. Certainly this may be taken at a crass literal level. It was early morning and the sun was not shining and so it was not yet daylight; but taken in the context of the Fourth Gospel with its penchant for wordplays, irony, and symbols, and given the benighted reaction of Mary to the discovery that the stone had been rolled away from the tomb, the darkness surely signifies spiritual as well as physical reality. Mary comes in darkness (as Nicodemus came to Jesus in John 3!). Since she is on her own and without the blessed perspective provided by the presence of Jesus Christ, the true Light of the world, we should not wonder at her lack of comprehension, indeed, her misunderstanding of what she sees.

Seeing, she does not see! Yet, she is not merely frozen by her lack of understanding; rather she turns to others with whom she is acquainted through a mutual fellowship with Jesus Christ. Her words to the disciples are peculiar, ''They have taken the Lord out of the tomb, and we do not know where they have laid him.'' Who are ''we'' in her statement? A traditional-historical reading of the text (which suggests that an earlier version of the story was more similar to the parallel accounts in the Synoptic Gospels and included the presence of other women with Mary at the tomb) does not explain the story as John tells it. Who are ''we'' here? Perhaps Mary is speaking for herself and the disciples at this point, for none of them understands at this time in the story.

Next, Simon Peter and the beloved disciple run to the tomb. They move farther than Mary, however, and enter the tomb. Now, not seeing the body of the crucified Lord, but seeing his abandoned burial garment, they do not understand but they believe. How remarkable that faith precedes full comprehension and how fortunate! We can only wonder exactly what the disciples believed as they stood in the empty tomb, but whatever it was, it gave them the strength to go home again. In other words, a measure of faith enabled the disciples, despite their limited comprehension, to begin to live again. They had been frozen by the seemingly tragic course of events composing Jesus' Passion, and now they became unstuck on the apparent failure of their hopes and dreams.

But the story continues. As Mary mourned, she experienced the grace of God in a most dramatic manner. Angels visit her in her sorrow, although they say nothing to alleviate her grief. And, then, the Lord himself comes to her. He begins with the question of the angels,

"Woman, why are you weeping?" And, he takes the conversation in a new direction, "Whom are you looking for?" The story is thus refocused from Mary's grief to the object of her sorrow, Jesus Christ. In the conversation, the Lord presents himself and explains himself to Mary, so that she is moved in the encounter from misunderstanding to belief and comprehension because of the revelatory presence of the Lord. Furthermore, as she earlier shared her ignorance, now she declares the truth of the Resurrection of Jesus Christ with the disciples.

In all these events we see that it is the presence and the activity of the Lord that bring the full transformation of life, which moves us into the true dynamics of Christian life and community. It is not merely from what we see and believe that we live as Christians. We form our existence through the real presence of Christ in our lives. All that we have which brings understanding to faith is what Christ gives to us.

The Gospel: *Mark 16:1-8*

"He Is Not Here!"

Setting. The brief, enigmatic story of the discovery of the empty tomb comes at the very end of the gospel according to Mark. The peculiarity of this ending motivated early Christian scribes to provide other, more elaborate endings for the story. Two different prominent endings are often included in translations of Mark either in the printed texts of the Gospel or as footnotes to the book. Our lesson seems, however, to be the oldest reliable ending for Mark, although its abrupt manner of closing the story has led many scholars to conclude that the original closing of the Gospel must have been lost very early in the circulation of this work.

Structure. The simple, straightforward action of the story gives shape to the account. Women go to the tomb to treat the body for burial. They wonder how they will get in, since a large stone sealed the grave. Upon discovering that the stone was rolled away, they enter the tomb and encounter a young man. They are frightened, but the young man speaks to them, giving them assurance and commissioning them to take a message to the disciples. The women depart in silence because of their fear and say "nothing to anyone" because of their fear. Ceremonial devotion, strange occurrences, and overwhelming fear are the obvious stages of the narrative; but at the heart of the story are the words of the young man.

Significance. Mark's story is not so obviously symbolic as is John's, although there is deep truth and irony in the account. The narrative is greatly understated. For example, what the women recognize that they cannot do (move the stone) has already been done. By whom? By the young man? Who is this fellow? His radiant garments suggest he is an angel, and if Matthew and Luke took their lead from Mark for composing their Gospels, they certainly understood this character in that way. The young man's knowledge of Jesus' fate and Jesus' earlier promises to the disciples (compare 16:7 with 14:28) clearly indicate divine capacities. Therefore, we must listen carefully to his words. They tell us plainly that Jesus Christ—who was crucified, dead, and buried—"has been raised" from the dead ("he is not here"). Furthermore, notice the unstated, but implicit, contrast in the declaration, "Look, there is the place they laid him." Human beings judged and executed Jesus, and human beings laid him to a seemingly final rest, but God is the one who acts finally in relation to Jesus Christ, and God raised him from the dead. The story of Jesus Christ is not ultimately about his fate in the hands of his enemies, rather it is the account of what God has done in and through him, of what God has even done for him.

The words of the young man continue. He speaks to the women, offering them comfort and assurance, then, commissioning them to active proclamation of the good news about·Jesus. Sermons that present messages about the women as the first evangelists (a popular theme that shows up with increasing regularity) are not based on Mark's account. Sadly, here, the women are abysmal failures. They live up to the standards set for them by other human beings, so that they act (or, better, fail to act) out of their own fear, not out of the strength of the good news given them. Recall that in Mark's Gospel Jesus confronted Peter, calling him "Satan" and declaring that he was thinking "human things," not God's. As Mark's Gospel now ends, the women illustrate the tendency of humans to take the wrong side in the conflict between God and Satan. Thus, in preaching from this text, the women are not the focus of the positive dimensions of the passage.

The good news about the Resurrection of Jesus Christ is a message about the goodness of God, goodness despite (perhaps even because of) the pitiful performance of humans. Yet one must be careful here, for the text does not launch a harangue against people. We must not become derailed in our reflection into making speeches either primarily for or against the women. After all, the good news is a message for the welfare of humanity, not our condemnation. The gospel is this: God's grace and power cannot be thwarted! God promises forgiveness despite our shortcomings. And, in Jesus Christ, especially in his Resurrection, we know that God makes good on his promises. Goodness prevails, thank goodness!

Easter Day: The Celebration

Mention was made in the earlier commentary on the season of Easter that in churches where the observance of the Vigil is not practicable, it may be possible to divide the parts of the Vigil up among the first three Sundays of Easter, with the Service of Light occurring at the sunrise service and the Service of the Word at the primary morning service on Easter Day. If that option is elected, and the ordering of the lessons is that of the Revised Common Lectionary (see *Year A: Lent/Easter*), then today's Old Testament lesson from Isaiah 25 and its response from Psalm 118 might be inserted between the readings from Exodus 14 and Isaiah 55. The lesson from Baruch could be omitted. Today's epistle reading from I Corinthians 15 would take the place of the reading from Romans 6, and the Gospel reading would be from Mark. Care needs to be taken to provide a brief but appropriate opening rite to introduce the series of lessons. The number of lessons may need to be reduced due to time constraints, but they should always include Exodus 14. While psalms are listed as responses to the lessons, hymns and anthems may also be used. Following are some suggestions of hymns that may be used in response to the lessons.

Gen. 1:1–2:4*a* (The Creation)
"All Things Bright and Beautiful"
"I Sing the Almighty Power of God"
"Morning Has Broken"

Gen. 7:1-5, 11-18; 8:6-18; 9:8-13 (The Flood)
"A Mighty Fortress Is Our God"
"Jesus, Savior, Pilot Me"
"O Love That Wilt Not Let Me Go"

Gen. 22:1-18 (The Sacrifice of Isaac)
"Beams of Heaven as I Go"
"How Firm a Foundation"
"We'll Understand It Better By and By"

Exodus 14:10-31; 15:20-21 (Crossing the Red Sea)
"Come, Ye Faithful, Raise the Strain"
"O Mary, Don't You Weep"

Isaiah 25:6-9 (The Divine Banquet)
"Christ Is Made the Sure Foundation"
"Come and Dine"
"This Is the Day the Lord Hath Made"

Isaiah 55:1-11 (The Assurance of Better Times)
"Come, Ye Disconsolate"
"Give to the Winds Thy Fears"

Ezekiel 36:24-28 (A New Heart and Spirit)
"As Pants the Hart for Cooling Streams"

Ezekiel 37:1-14 (The Valley of Dry Bones)
"Breathe on Me, Breath of God"
"In the Bulb There Is a Flower"
"Revive Us Again"

Zephaniah 3:14-20 (A Song of Joy)
"Joy to the World" (This is not a misprint! There is nothing in the text of this hymn that restricts it to Christmas. Use of it at this time may be helpful in making the point that the whole Christian year is related to the Paschal mystery.)

It may be preferable to mix hymns and psalms and anthems to provide variety to the responses.

Psalm 118:19-24 can be adapted as a call to worship, although the ancient formula of ''Christ is risen!'' with its response, ''The Lord is risen indeed!'' should not be ignored during the Great Fifty Days. The Old Testament lesson suggests that the Eucharist may be an appropriate part of today's celebration since it is the Christian's anticipation of the heavenly banquet.

Second Sunday of Easter

Texts from Acts and Psalms

Acts 4:32-35 is a challenging idealization of community within the early church. Psalm 133 provides "wise" reflection on the same theme.

The Lesson: Acts 4:32-35

Sharing: Guilt or Eschatology?

Setting. Acts 4:32-35 introduces the fourth cycle of events in the book of Acts. These four cycles include: (1) the Ascension of Jesus and the promise of the Holy Spirit (Acts 1), (2) Pentecost (Acts 2), (3) the controversy surrounding the healing of the lame man in the Temple (Acts 3:1–4:31), and (4) the ongoing development of the early church community (Acts 4:32–5:16). Each of these sections is meant to demonstrate the power of the Resurrection, first, through the apostles and, second, in the community of believers. For example, Pentecost describes the miracle of the outpouring of the Holy Spirit on the Apostles (2:1-13), it includes Peter's sermon (2:14-41), and concludes with a summary statement concerning the life of the community (2:42-47). The third cycle (3:1–4:31) follows the same pattern of miracle, apostolic sermon, and portrait of the community: It begins with a miracle demonstrating the power of the resurrection through the Apostles (3:1-10), a sermon by Peter (3:11-26) along with the arrest of Peter and John (4:1-22), and a summary description of the community of believers at prayer (4:23-31). The fourth cycle, of which 4:32-35 provides the introduction, departs from the pattern of the previous two cycles in order to focus exclusively on the life of the community. The two previous cycles underscore how this unit must also be interpreted in the larger context of the miracle of the Resurrection, and how it is demonstrated—first, through the Apostles and, second, in the community of believers.

Structure. The text modulates between reference to the community ("the whole group" in vv. 32, and third person plural references ["all," "them," "they"] in vv. 33*b*, 34, 35) and the apostles (vv. 33*a*, 35). These different points of focus provide insight for a three-part structure in the text. Verse 32 is a description of the community sharing their possessions. Verse 33 roots this activity in the power of the Resurrection as it is proclaimed by the apostles. And vv. 34-35 show the interaction of community and apostles in the distribution of property.

Significance. This text is a hot potato for Christians in the North American context, for a number of reasons. First, upon initial reading it looks to be communistic, which presents a clash of values even in a post-cold war context. Second, even without political ideology, a sermon advocating the communitarian ideal of giving up all private possessions—especially for Christians who live in an individualistic, capitalistic society—must be interpreted as either a naive belief in the imminent parousia of Jesus or economic suicide. And, third, preaching about possessions in a consumer-oriented society strikes too close to home. We are all vulnerable at this point, and thus sermons on idealized communal life in Acts are guilt trips before a word is stated. The central aim in preaching this text, therefore, is to underscore how the ideal of community in Acts is not rooted in human guilt, but in the power of the Resurrection.

Several points are important for preaching on this important text. One, the ideal of community is intimately woven with the power of apostolic proclamation concerning the power of the Resurrection. Two, the ideal of community is not presented as a law in Acts 4:32-35, but as the result of grace (v. 33*b*). If it were a law, guilt would be as good a motive for compliance as anything else. Three, the ideal of community is not national or societal but religious. The text presents a sharp conflict between Christ and culture, between the worshiping community and the larger world. Four, the conflict is not within individual Christians, but between communities.

The text helps us remember that the Church is an eschatological community rooted in the Resurrection of Jesus. Its standards, therefore, are in conflict with the larger culture in which it exists. Christians live with a foot in both of these worlds. Maturity in the faith, according to Luke, is measured by the degree to which Christian communities can learn to stand on the foot that is in the Church. The paradox of Acts 4:32-35 is that when communities do in fact mature in the faith by exploring standards of community that are at odds with their larger culture, they see that their actions were really a divine gift. Sharing in the Church is not a human law, it is a gift of grace. Consequently, such activity within the Church does not appease human guilt, it affirms the Resurrection of Christ.

The Response: *Psalm 133*

In Praise of Community

Setting. The influence of the wisdom tradition among the scribes of Israel is especially apparent in the opening verse of Psalm 133. The initial phrase, "how very good" is characteristic of the wisdom literature. There is debate whether this psalm is sacred or profane, whether it is about the everyday life of the community at large, or about the worshiping community. Those who favor the former reading interpret the reference to Aaron in v. 2 and Zion in v. 3 as later additions.

Structure. The psalm opens with a wisdom saying about the goodness of community (v. 1) and two analogies (vv. 2 and 3), which are meant to describe, by means of imagery, just how good the community can be.

Significance. The arguments for interpreting Psalm 133 as a profane hymn about community clearly go against the present images in the text. The first analogy centers on Aaron, the high priest, and the second analogy emphasizes the cult site of Zion. No matter what the prehistory of this psalm may have been, in its present form it is a celebration of religious community within the context of worship. And, as such, it accentuates the imagery from Acts 4:32-35, and even underscores the message in that text, that community among beievers is a gift from God (namely, the result of God's blessing).

New Testament Texts

The lessons bring together the first of a series of sequential readings from I John and the continuation of the materials from the Easter stories in the gospel according to John. Remarkably the text from the epistle refers to that which "we have heard . . . seen with our eyes . . . looked at and touched with our hands," whereas in the course of the passage(s) from the Gospel, Thomas demands to "see the mark of the nails in his hands, [to] put [his] finger in the mark of the nails and [his] hand in [the risen Jesus'] side" so that he can believe.

The Epistle: *I John 1:1–2:2*

Life in the Light of God

Setting. Our lesson comprises the first sections of I John. Although we call this writing an epistle, it is not a letter. It is an address to a community from which a group has gone out, separating itself from the original congregation. The separatists now pose a threat to the original community, and the author of I John responds to that danger by denouncing the detached group and by offering a course of acceptable teaching. The address is highly repetitious and is written in very ambiguous Greek. Thus, despite its apparent simplicity I John is a subtle document that requires careful attention. All translations of I John are highly interpretive, and use of a reliable critical commentary is practically necessary.

Structure. Commentators perceive that I John opens with a prologue (1:1-4), after which there are two major sections of meditation, both beginning with the line, "This is the message" (1:5–3:10; 3:11–5:12). The address concludes with an epilogue (5:13-21). The verses of our lesson come both from the prologue and from the first two portions of the first major section of the address (1:5-7; 1:8–2:2). The themes of these segments are (1) testimony to the manifestation of the divine, (2) walking in the light, and (3) awareness of and opposition to sin. These items are intimately related to one another in the thought of the author of I John.

116

Significance. The prologue of this epistle is reminiscent of the prologue to the Fourth Gospel, which itself evokes memories of the opening lines of Genesis. The Gospel, however, celebrated "the Word" made flesh, whereas here we find the phrase "the Word of Life," which emphasizes life more than Word, as becomes clear in v. 2. Indeed, I John is more concerned with *the manifestation of life* than with *life itself.* The author recalls this manifestation in order to be able to refer, in turn, to the testimony concerning the manifestation of life. That testimony had been given to those addressed in this epistle.

The beginning celebrated in this prologue is not the beginning of creation. Rather, it seems to be the beginning of the life of Christian faith that came into being in relation to the manifestation of life in Jesus Christ. The author brings up "the beginning" to call the members of the community back to the foundation of their corporate faith. Recent developments in the life of the community had caused dissension, leading to schism. Now, I John calls those in the community back to their origins in the life of the congregation and reminds them that their existence together is based on the testimony given them concerning the eternal life that was manifested to earlier eyewitnesses. The call to remember beginnings is an appeal to renew confidence in the earlier testimony upon which the community was founded. The power of eternal life is mediated to the community in and through the testimony of the eyewitnesses who experienced the life manifested from the Father. The thought of the prologue is twisted and difficult, even opaque; but it is a reminder that in any generation the Christian community inherits its foundation from those who have gone before in the faith.

Upon the foundation of shared faith, we are called to a distinctive manner of life. I John declares that God is Light, and that as believers we walk in the light. The vision of Christian faith is the vision of God, given to the community of faith in and through what God has done for us in Jesus Christ. We are shown God's will in Christ, and we are called to live our lives in faithful compliance to that will. We are not, however, merely playing by the rules or living up to a revealed standard. The life we live is one of true fellowship with God. God revealed God's self in Jesus Christ in order to call us into a personal relationship with God, and in that relationship there is an enabling fellowship that issues in a Godlike quality of life ("practicing the truth"—see v. 6).

The author knows that sadly, despite the joy of divine fellowship, human believers are still sinners. Christian faith does not deny sin, and it does not condone sin; rather it takes seriously that God has called us out of our sinfulness and has made provision for our forgiveness. Thus we are called to repentance and to the genuine experience of forgiveness—both of which lead us away from sin. Yet even as we fail in faith and lapse into sin, there is the promise of forgiveness in Jesus Christ.

The Gospel: *John 20:19-31*

Peace, Commission, Doubts, Blessing, and Belief

Setting. This lesson follows immediately on the verses composing last week's Gospel lesson. Readers might consult that previous discussion of setting in preparation for this week's text.

Structure. This lesson contains three items: two distinct but related scenes and a formal word of closure related to everything that has come before in the Gospel. First, vv. 19-23 recount the appearance of the risen Jesus to the disciples as they were gathered behind closed doors on the evening of the first Easter. Then, building off this account, vv. 24-29 tell of Thomas's absence when Jesus originally appeared to the disciples, of Thomas's doubts, and of Jesus' subsequent appearance to him in the presence of the other disciples. Finally, vv. 30-31 make what is surely one of the finest closing statements ever offered for a book (except the Gospel does not conclude here!).

Significance. The presence of the risen Lord comes in a miraculous manner and grants to the disciples the "peace" of the Lord. There is no rebuke because of the fear that has paralyzed the disciples and driven them into hiding. Instead of a negative tone, the appearance is purely positive in character; it means and brings peace. The reaction of the disciples is appropriate, they are overjoyed at the sight of the risen Jesus. Their joy is far more than a static or selfish experience that means only good feelings; it is the disposition to which Christ issues a commission to service. The good news of the reality of Christ's

Resurrection, the overpowering revelation of the irrepressible nature of the love of God, is the foundation of a divine call to faithful service. Christ commissions the disciples, making of them real Christians—a term that in its origin meant "little Christs." As God sent Jesus, so now the risen Lord Jesus Christ sends the disciples to do the will and the work of God in the world. As the light of the world Christ came into darkness, and though in the death of Jesus it appeared that darkness had overcome the light, now through the Resurrection we are shown that the light still shines in the darkness. Indeed, the light that shines calls forth new "points of light" as Christ calls the disciples into the same kind of divinely directed service that he had given his whole self to do. Yet, notice here, as is ever the case in relation to the gospel call to service, the disciples (and we) are not merely told to get the job done. The disciples (and we) are given the powerful gift of the Holy Spirit. We receive God's own power and presence for doing the work to which our risen Lord Jesus Christ directs us.

In the next scene we find that reasonable doubts do not disqualify us for discipleship. Instead our doubts are addressed by the risen Lord who alone is capable of allaying our apprehensions. Today there are many who share Thomas's reservations. Many would insist that the favor granted to Thomas gave him an unfair advantage, for who would not believe after having seen the risen Lord. It is well, however, to reflect carefully in relation to this text. While we do not share Thomas's seeming advantage, we also do not have the serious handicap that confounded his capacity to believe the good news that Christ is risen. We have never known Christ in the flesh. We have never seen him crucified, dead, and buried; and today we live in a world where for nearly two thousand years believers have been sustained by their conviction of the reality of the Resurrection and of Christ's real presence in their lives. For us the reality of lives of faith are as much evidence of Christ's presence as was his standing before Thomas in the company of the other disciples after they had known him crucified. Yet, be that as it may, in this lesson Christ's own words are spoken through the text to us as a word of sacred assurance, "Blessed are those who have not seen and yet have come to believe."

As the twentieth chapter of John comes to its conclusion (perhaps recording the ending of an earlier edition of the Gospel—see a commentary on this Gospel) the author turns directly to the readers and states the purposes of his writing. The stories in John's Gospel are testimony to the work of God in Jesus Christ, and they are offered to inspire faith in Jesus Christ. In turn, that faith means life in his name for those who believe.

Easter 2: The Celebration

The Gospel reading for today contains the Johannine equivalent of Pentecost, the narrative of the gift of the Spirit by Jesus upon the disciples on the evening of the first Easter Day. What is particularly noteworthy in John's account is how intimately the gift of the Spirit is tied to the power to forgive sins. Roman Catholic commentators have been inclined to see this as the first ordination and the institution of a priestly cult with a primary responsibility to pronounce absolution. Protestants tend to see it as an action of Christ in relation to the whole Church, a commission to proclaim the divine judgment and forgiveness, which the work of Christ has pronounced upon the whole world. Both Catholics and Protestants generally agree on the importance of confessing sins as a part of their liturgical life, but it is not always easy to find agreement about what it means. Although there is a general absolution given in Mass, Catholics encourage separate sacramental confession or reconciliation. It is not unusual to find Protestant liturgies that include a prayer of confession, but which have not even "words of assurance," let alone a declaration of pardon or form of absolution!

Liturgical action should seek to hold in tension both an understanding of absolution as a responsibility given to the whole Church in relation to the world and one another and given to individuals in ordination as a sign in and to the Church of what the Church should be doing in the world. It is this understanding that the Lima Liturgy seeks to incorporate in its absolution formula:

> Almighty God gave Jesus Christ to die for us and for the sake of Christ forgives us all our sins. As a called and ordained minister of the Church and by the authority of Jesus Christ, I therefore declare to you the entire forgiveness of all your sins, in the name of the Father, and of the Son, and of the Holy Spirit. (Lima Liturgy in *Baptism and Eucharist: Ecumenical Convergence in Celebration*, Max Thurian and Geoffrey Wainwright [Grand Rapids: Eerdman's, 1983], p. 249), Copyright © 1983 WCC Publications.

Here absolution is based in God's saving activity in Christ and is only exercised by the minister as Christ's representative and proclaimer of the gospel. Another form of absolution in recent liturgies is reciprocal between pastor and people with each saying to the other in turn, "In the name of Jesus Christ you are forgiven." Other formulas can be found in the Presbyterian *Service for the Lord's Day: Supplemental Liturgical Resource 1* (Louisville: Westminster/John Knox, 1984).

For those traditions that prefer "Words of Assurance" to a declaratory form of absolution, today's epistle lesson provides one set (I John 2:1*b*-2) which has appeared in the Anglican "Comfortable Words" since the sixteenth century.

Charles Wesley provides two texts based on the Gospel reading that may be used liturgically. The following lines may serve as an introit or choral call to worship:

> Jesus, we thy promise claim,
> We are met in thy great name;
> In the midst do thou appear,
> Manifest thy presence here!
> Sanctify us, Lord, and bless!
> Breathe thy Spirit, give thy peace;
> Thou thyself within us move,
> Make our feast a feast of love.

These may be sung to the tune Easter Hymn, with the "Alleluia" after each line.

The following, sung to any powerful common meter tune, may be used as a response to the reading of the Gospel:

> Breathe on us, Lord, in this our day,
> And these dry bones shall live;
> Speak peace into our hearts, and say,
> "The Holy Ghost receive!"

Third Sunday of Easter

Texts from Acts and Psalms

Acts 3:12-19 is part of Peter's second sermon to Israel. Psalm 4 is a prayer of confidence during a time of persecution.

The Lesson: *Acts 3:12-19*

Two Perspectives on Jesus

Setting. See the commentary under setting from last week for a brief overview of the four cycles that make up the opening chapters of Acts. This is the second episode in which a sermon by Peter plays a prominent role (see also Peter's Pentecost sermon in 2:14-41). In this episode the healing of a lame man in the Temple (3:1-10) and the astonishment of the crowd (3:11) provide the occasion for Peter to address fellow worshipers in the Temple concerning the power of the resurrection of Jesus (3:12-26), which eventually leads to his and John's arrest, thus providing the setting for the continuation of Peter's sermon (4:1-22). The cycle closes with an account of their release and a picture of the church at prayer (4:23-31).

Structure. The initial speech by Peter overlaps the boundaries of the lectionary text in both directions. The opening words in v. 12, "When Peter saw it" presupposes the astonished response of the audience in v. 11. Moreover, the call for repentance in v. 19 does not end the speech. Rather it continues through v. 26. The interpreter must decide whether the boundaries of the lectionary will be followed. At the very least, v. 11 should be added to the reading to provide minimal context ("astonishment") for the discourse by Peter.

The speech of Peter separates into two parts, which are clearly marked with separate introductions. Note how v. 12 includes a direct address, "You Israelites," and how v. 17 marks a transition with the words, "And now, friends." Interpretation will follow this two-part structure, vv. 11-16 and vv. 17-19.

Significance. The internal structure of this speech is meant to highlight a contrast between two different perceptions of Jesus: Israel's and God's. The astonishment of those in the Temple at the miracle performed by Peter and John provides the key for the series of contrasts. Peter's central point in vv. 11-16 can be stated as follows: for the Temple crowd to think that Peter and John are miracle workers is not primarily a misinterpretation of them or their power as much as it is a misinterpretation of Jesus. This point provides a frame to the opening section of the sermon. Note how Peter denies the power to heal in v. 12 and locates it in the name of Jesus in v. 16. The verses in between provide content to the name of Jesus through contrast. To the people Jesus was someone to be rejected and marked for death. From God's point of view Jesus was the suffering servant, the Holy One, and the Righteous One, who was raised from the dead. From one perspective Jesus is powerless and from the other perspective Jesus is the "author of life." The difference between these opposite poles is faith in his name (v. 16). Those who are astonished symbolize the powerlessness of Jesus. The healed lame man, Peter, and John symbolize the power of Jesus' name. The difference between the two perspectives is minimal, which prompts the second part of the speech.

A new introduction draws Peter and the audience in a much closer orbit, when he describes those around him as "friends" in v. 17. Even with the new introduction, the contrast between people and God continues. The theological reflection, however, moves to another level. No longer does Peter summarize events of Jesus' Passion from two different points of view. Instead, he interrelates the two actions. Israel, we are told, acted in ignorance, while God used this blindness to fulfill prophecy. The result is that suffering is an essential characteristic of the ministry of Jesus. The two perspectives can be brought together by a simple change of direction: hence the call to repent in v. 19.

This is a difficult text to preach, especially in light of two thousand years of anti-Semitism. Luke is clearly concerned with the historical problem of Israel being the chosen people of God, and their rejection of Jesus. This concern is an immediate problem for him and cannot be minimalized in the text, but it is not a fruitful avenue for preaching in the contemporary context, where Jewish-Christian relations have taken on a very different role. Perhaps a better path to take in preaching this text is to place your church in the context of the astonished Israelites addressed by Peter. In many ways this is closer to the social context of the text where Israel is functioning as the established people of God who are put in the role of being blinded to a new action of God. The central questions to be addressed in such an Easter sermon are (1) the power of blindness or ignorance that results in us either not seeing the miracles of God or being surprised and misinterpreting them when they happen, (2) the power that exists in the name of Jesus, (3) the minimal difference between accessing this power and living in blindness, and (4) the ease by which this gap can be bridged (for example, by repentance).

The Response: *Psalm 4*

Unjust Suffering

Setting. Psalm 4 has been categorized as both an individual lament and as a psalm of confidence. These two different classifications are worthy of a moment of reflection, for they illustrate how the act of lamenting is itself confession of confidence in God. Hence, the two categories are frequently mixed in psalm studies. The imagery of the psalm underscores how the threat of enemies to the psalmist is still immediate (vv. 2-5) even though God has declared that the sufferer is innocent (v. 3). How is the faithful person to act in such a situation?

Structure. The structure of the psalm is not clear. One key for determining the movement in the psalm is to follow who is addressed and who is speaking. With this clue to the structure, the opening verse stands apart with the direct plea for God to answer the psalmist. In vv. 2-4 the psalmist addresses those who are persecuting her ("you people" in v. 2 and "when you are disturbed" in v. 4). Verse 5 could either be a continuation of the psalmist addressing her persecutors, or it could be a priest addressing the psalmist. The psalm ends with an address to God in which two different attitudes are described: those who are impatient with God (v. 6) and the psalmist who is trusting in God (vv. 7-8).

Significance. The psalm explores the experience of unjust suffering. The oppressors are described in v. 2 as persons intent on accusing the psalmist, even though the psalmist has already been vindicated by God (v. 3), and has found sanctuary in the Temple ("You gave me room when I was in distress" v. 1). This situation provides the occasion for the psalmist to explore how faith in God is meant to function as trust in such contexts. Verse 4 introduces the motif of trust as a statement either by the psalmist or by a priest in the Temple. The closing verses (vv. 7-8) illustrate how trust must function in the life of a believer during the anguish of unjust suffering. The psalm provides commentary on the larger context of Acts 3:1–4:31, where the miracle of healing the lame man will eventually result in the arrest of Peter and John.

New Testament Texts

This week, while we continue to draw epistle lessons from I John for the weeks after Easter, we diverge from the gospel according to John to take our Gospel lesson from the final chapter of Luke. The story from Luke is highly reminiscent of last week's Gospel lesson, for again we read of an appearance of the risen Jesus to the disciples and again we hear him say, "Peace be with you" (although there is a textual problem related to this line) and again he refers to the evidence of his crucifixion, which he bears in his resurrected form.

The Epistle: *I John 3:1-7*

On Being "Children of God"

Setting. The verses of the epistle lesson are the last three verses of a section that forms a meditation on the theme "children of God" (2:28–3:3) and the first four verses of a section calling the "children" of the author's community to avoid sin (3:4-10). This lesson is located in the first major section of this epistle (1:5–3:10), which works with the metaphor of "walking in God's light" to reflect upon the meaning and the manner of living according to God's will.

Structure. The lesson is a series of statements that (1) recognize the love of God that makes children of God into believers, (2) explain the indifference and animosity of "the world" toward God's children, (3) declare both the present reality and the future hope of being God's children, (4) remind the "children" of the promised future revelation of the Son, (5) call those who hope in Jesus to Christlike purity, (6) define sin, (7) inform the "children" that sin is not a characteristic of Christian life, (8) advise the readers to avoid those who would lead them into sin, and (9) admonish them to live righteous lives. A nine point sermon is impossible, but a selection from these elements can enhance the sermon's content.

Significance. The text opens with the words, "See what love the Father has given us." The reference to "love" is christological, for the love of God given to humanity was none other than God's Son, Jesus. God's gift of Jesus has had transforming effects on those who believe in the Son, so that they are now called part of God's family. This new identity is a description of the real transformation of lives through the establishment of a new relationship with God. Yet, as the passage admits, the reality of the relationship does not alter all of life's experiences, for "the world" (that is, those outside God's family and in opposition to both the Son and God's children) does not recognize the relationship.

Nevertheless, the elder boldly states the reality of Christian "childhood" and goes on to remind the readers that the future holds even more than they are currently experiencing. There is both a realized and a future dimension to the life of faith, and these dimensions are complementary in that the future gives amplified meaning to the present. Moreover, the future hope of the life of faith in the present is not an ambiguous wish; rather, it is the clear expectation of the future revelation of the Son with the attendant belief that his revelation will itself effect the ultimate transformation of believers into complete children of God.

The present status of believers as God's children and their future hope of the revelation of the Son and their own full and final transformation has real ethical meaning for the present. In both the new identity and the future hope are a call to a thoroughly Christlike existence in the present. Purity of life (or sanctity) is the proper preparation for full childhood, for believers are called now to be as they will be when the Son is revealed. In this thinking, Christian hope is not pie-in-the-sky; rather, it is the substance and motivation of real life in the present world. A sermon or meditation on this lesson should deal with the God-givenness of "childhood," the christological basis of our new identity, and the continuity between current Christian living and the future expectation of the realization of God redemption.

Furthermore, there is a dimension of this lesson that warns and admonishes as well as instructs. Sin is taken seriously, and it is not to be given a place in the lives of believers. One excellent precaution against sin is to be on guard against those who themselves would lead believers astray. Rather than have dealings with such persons, the believer is to affirm and pursue actively that which is right. The standard of righteousness is declared to be Jesus Christ in v. 7, where the "he" in the phrase "he is righteousness" is Christ. The children of God are to become like the child of God, conforming their lives to his as the way of righteousness.

The Gospel: *Luke 24:36b-48*

Resurrection, Real Presence, and Responsible Discipleship

Setting. Luke 24 focuses on the Resurrection of Jesus by presenting four distinct scenes: the account of the empty tomb (vv. 1-12); the story of Jesus' appearance to two disciples on the road to Emmaus (vv. 13-35); the report of Jesus' appearance to the disciples assembled in Jerusalem (vv. 36-48); and the Ascension (24:50-53). The first scene has parallels in Matthew, Mark, and John. The third scene (our lesson) seems similar in part to John 20:19-23. And the fourth scene has a vague parallel in Acts 1. The similarities, dissimilarities, and variety in the Resurrection stories point to the selectivity and deliberateness of the evangelists in formulating their narratives.

Structure. Our lesson is a single scene that unfolds in three parts. First, the risen Jesus appears and declares "peace" to the disciples and exhibits the reality of his Resurrection from the dead. Second, building on the presentation of the evidence of the reality of his death and Resurrection, Jesus eats fish before the watching disciples. And, third, Jesus explains the significance of his death and Resurrection and commissions the disciples to be his witnesses. In doing this he promises them they will be "clothed with power from on high," words anticipating the forthcoming events of Pentecost that will be narrated in Luke's second volume, Acts.

Significance. Striking ideas dance in the verses of our lesson. In the disciples we see the peculiar truth of disabling joy ("in their joy they were disbelieving"). In the words and acts of Jesus we find that the risen Lord is no phantom. In Christ's manner of teaching we find the theme of prophecy and fulfillment scored once again, and we see the foundation for the work of Christ and the mission of the Church set and authorized even in the Old Testament. And, in the promise of the risen Jesus that the disciples will receive power from on high, we learn that it is God's power, not merely human energy, that actualizes Christian ministry. Other ideas are inherent in the text, but let us dwell on three crucial dimensions of the lesson.

First, the nature of death and resurrection are shown implicitly in our text. Death and resurrection do not mean absconding from responsible existence. The risen Jesus was real and recognizable. George Bernard Shaw said he could imagine no fate more horrible than remaining himself forever. Our lesson informs him (and us) that he had no cause to worry. The good news of the story is that in resurrection there is a genuine transformation of the self, but it is not a change into a dreamy fantastic state that would be so totally different as to be completely discontinuous with the lives we have lived as real human beings. Resurrection life is God's own mystery, but we hope for it as life continuous with but different from the one we now know.

Second, at an earlier point in Luke 24 we saw how the risen Lord came to table with two disciples and how it was there that they finally recognized his presence. In this story he continues the meal-fellowship with those whom he called and loved. The eating of fish seems to make several points. Obviously it underscores that the risen Lord was not a ghost. But the fish itself, an early and prominent symbol for discipleship, points to the real fellowship with the risen Lord that is enjoyed by believers. The meal recalls the feeding of the multitude (see Luke 9:12-17), Mary's praise for the Lord, "He has filled the hungry with good things'' (Luke 1:53), and the steady series of meals Jesus shared with those to whom and among whom he ministered. That Jesus is alive is celebrated, proclaimed, and experienced by the community of faith in their table fellowship in his name. Thus, in Acts we find the disciples ''breaking bread'' as a community of believers. The reality of Christ's Resurrection is itself the foundation for the community's life together.

Third, the death and the Resurrection of Jesus lead to the mission of the disciples. The disciples are directed into their work by the command of the risen Lord, but the precedent for their labors is found in the expressed will of the Lord recorded in the Old Testament and the power for their service comes from God alone. Christ lived, worked, died, and was raised in fulfillment of God's work and promises. In Jesus God accomplished salvation for humanity on a universal scale, and now through the risen Lord, God enlists, instructs, and empowers the disciples to extend the liberating ministry ''to all nations.''

Preaching done in relation to this lesson will have to find a focus, for the text is filled with riches that could inspire countless sermons. One should not try to preach everything in this passage at once. Perhaps only part of the lesson should be used, or even a selected theme from the lesson can stand as the topic of the sermon.

Easter 3: The Celebration

The above exegetical comment on Acts has pointed to the difficulty involved when a lesson is drawn from a larger narrative and is in part dependent for its interpretation upon understanding that wider context. What is true for preaching is also true for an intelligent reading and hearing of the lesson in the liturgy. The reader might appreciate the context in which it appears if the lesson is to be read with understanding, and the congregation needs to discern the background against which the particular action in the lesson is occurring.

This points to the need for persons who read Scripture (or any other portions of the liturgy) to have prepared themselves in advance for the task. The widespread use of lay readers in recent years, while laudable on the one hand, can also contribute to a lack of reverence for the

Scriptures if their reading is seen to be so unimportant that a reader may be chosen at the last moment and have thrust before her eyes a passage of Scripture that she has never seen before. We should not forget that by the third century the duty of scripture reading was so important that individuals were ordained to the office of lector or reader. At their ordination they were admonished by the bishop as follows:

> Endeavor to read the word of God, that is, the sacred lessons, distinctly and intelligibly, without any mistake or falsification, so that the faithful may understand and be edified, and so that the truth of the divine lessons may not, through your carelessness, be lost for the instruction of the hearers. (*The Rites of Ordination and Episcopal Consecration* [Washington, D.C.: National Conference of Catholic Bishops, 1967], p. 11)

Those who read lessons in church should know in advance what those lessons are and from which version or particular book (lectern Bible, and so on) they will be reading, so they will be familiar with the tools and can give themselves wholly to the reading. Training for lectors should involve familiarity with the background of the lessons and their context as well as the techniques of public speech and reading.

For lessons such as today's from Acts, introductory commentary may be in order so that the congregation can listen more appreciatively to what is being read. The intent of the commentary is to provide a context for hearing rather than to preach a minisermon or tell the congregation what the reader thinks they should be hearing. The liturgical reading of lessons is one thing; preaching is another. They are interdependent but should not be confused. As with the Trinity, we should neither confound their persons nor divide their substance! Today's lesson might be introduced as follows:

Peter and John were going to the Temple when they were stopped by a lame beggar asking for alms. They said they had no money, but they cured him "in the name of Jesus Christ." Word quickly spread of this miracle, and a great crowd gathered to see both the man they had all known to be lame and the men who had cured him. It is at this point that today's lesson begins.

[a brief pause]

"When Peter saw it . . ."

Notice that there is no reason to cite the passage being read. It will probably appear in the day's bulletin, but even if it doesn't, the important thing is to have the people listen, not distract them with information they don't need at the moment. The custom of having people follow along in pew Bibles (or their own) privatizes what should be a communal happening and, in these days of varied translations, can create a liturgical Babel.

Fourth Sunday of Easter

Texts from Acts and Psalms

Acts 4:5-12 is a portion of Peter's sermon before the rulers of Israel after he and John were arrested for preaching about the Resurrection of Jesus in the Temple. Psalm 23 is the familiar prayer of confidence and thanksgiving in the protective power of God.

The Lesson: *Acts 4:5-12*

The Name of Jesus

Setting. Acts 4:5-12 follows directly from the lesson for last week. The healing of the lame man and the reaction of astonishment by the crowd in the Temple provided the occasion for an intital sermon by Peter. The content of this sermon on the Resurrection of Jesus gets him and John arrested by the Jewish leaders. The setting of Acts 4:5-12 is before the council of Jewish leaders on the following day, and the lectionary text is part of Peter's response to the leaders. The central theme of his speech is the meaning of the name of Jesus.

Structure. The larger structure of the confrontation between Peter and John and the Jewish leaders includes Acts 4:1-22. This section separates into three parts: the arrest (vv. 1-4), the appearance before the council on the following day (vv. 5-12), and the leader's evaluation of Peter and John and their release (vv. 13-22). The lectionary text is the confrontation between the apostles and the Jewish leaders, and it consists primarily of a speech by Peter. The speech is prompted by the question in v. 7: ''By what power or by what name did you do this?'' Peter's response in vv. 8-12 is an attempt to answer the question concerning the meaning of the name of Jesus.

Significance. The religious background of the text assumes a long-established belief in the ancient Near East that names have inherent power. Note how power and name are combined in the question of v. 7. This belief is deeply rooted in Israel. Recall, for example, how important naming is in the Jacob cycle of stories in Genesis (see the commentary on these stories for Year A). These stories illustrate that names are not arbitrary designations for people as they are in contemporary culture. Rather, names embody the fundamental character of a person. Jacob is so named because he is a "supplanter" or, perhaps better, a trickster. When he encounters God at the Jabbok River and is transformed, he requires a new name to embody his new character, Israel, "one who struggles with God." The Jacob cycle of stories illustrates the belief that there is power in names. This power also applied to gods. To know the name of a god was to have access into the very character of that god. An example of this belief is evident in the Babylonian creation mythology, *Enuma Elish*. This mythology celebrates the creative power of Marduk, the central deity of the Babylonians, and it ends by giving a list of fifty of his names. These names provide both insight and access into Marduk's character for worshipers.

This belief in the power of names and the control that worshipers could have in knowing a god's name is why the name of God is so elusive in the Old Testament. Read the stories that surround the name of God in Exodus 3–4, where a name for God is never really given, and instead the verb *to be* in the third masculine singular is offered. Jehovah (The King James Version's attempt at the name), Yahweh (the estimate of modern biblical scholars), or the Lord (the NRSV solution) all illustrate the problems that the verb-name HE IS (Hebrew, *yhwh* given in Exodus 3:15) presents for anyone who may wish to know the name of God. The elusive verb-name for God underscores how Yahweh could not be controlled through a name. In fact, the name actually confronts us with a question: HE IS what?

In Acts 4 a miracle has occurred. Such miracles are signs of divine action through people (see 4:16). The obvious question, therefore, is the one addressed to Peter and John in 4:7: "By what power or by what name did you do this?" Peter's response must be interpreted as heresy in the larger context of Judaism because he names God, and in so doing he provides an answer to what should remain a question: HE IS what? Peter's response is that HE IS Jesus. Peter's response goes to the heart of Christianity—which is that in Christ, God has done the unthinkable by providing a name that gives worshipers power and access into the divine. Peter quotes Psalm 118:22 to describe the implications of this action. The power of the name Jesus is nothing less than the cornerstone of a whole new reality. Such a belief in the power of names may strike us as primitive, but we access this power every time we end prayer with the words "In Jesus' name, amen."

The Response: *Psalm 23*

The Security of Anointing

Setting. This is one of the most familiar psalms in Scripture. We all learn it as children, and over time the pastoral imagery of God as our shepherd becomes almost romantic. This is unfortunate, because even though Psalm 23 is about security, it is not a romantic psalm. In fact the background of the psalm is just the reverse. Danger is looming large for the singer of this prayer song. Verse 4 provides the setting, and it includes images of death and evil. The confession of God's security must be seen against this background.

Structure. The psalm could be separated into three parts: vv. 1-2, confession of God as shepherd; vv. 3-4, a description of the wanderer; and vv. 5-6, a description of God as host. This outline is forced because vv. 3-4 are not necessarily a description of wandering as much as they are a description of threat. In view of this, a two-part division might better convey the message of the psalm: vv. 1-4, a confession of God as shepherd in the context of threat; and vv. 5-6, a confession of divine security in the context of the worshiping community.

Significance. The significance of Psalm 23 is in the contrast between the two parts, which underscores the security of God's anointing. The first section of the psalm divides between a description of God as shepherd in vv. 1-3 and the situation of the psalmist in v. 4. God is a shepherd, who is able to lead, restore, and provide nurture (vv. 1-3), even in the darkest situations (v. 4), because he is never absent from us. Note the only direct address to God in vv. 1-4 occurs in v. 4 ("for you are with me"). This confession underscores how God is present even when we have moved to the outer reaches of God's domain and thus come under the shadow of death. The scene changes abruptly, however, in vv. 5-6 from threat and death to a banquet as the worshiper moves into the very presence of God within the sanctuary. Here the metaphors for God shift from shepherd in a threatening situation to host within the security of a home. God prepares a banquet for worshiper and enemies. This shift in imagery from shepherd to host underscores how worship is where our real security lies. As one commentator on this psalm states, worship is the sphere where God's protection is most readily available. This reality is underscored through the motif of anointing in v. 5, which gives rise to a whole new perspective on the part of the worshiper. The threat of enemies in pursuit through a valley of death shifts in v. 6 to the pursuit of goodness and mercy in the Temple of God—even while the enemies look on. The confession of the worshiper in v. 6 is anything but a romantic vision, for it goes against our notions of security.

New Testament Texts

The lessons return to the selected sequential readings from I John and John. In the text from the epistle we hear about the divine commands to Christians to believe in Jesus Christ and to love one another as children of God in the way that Christ himself loved us. Here, Christ is the object of Christian faith and the model of Christian love. The passage from John's Gospel is a christological speech about Christ as the good shepherd. From this passage we learn primarily about the person and work of our Lord, but implicit in the images and statements of the text are vital lessons about Christian life.

The Epistle: *I John 3:16-24*

What It Means to Love

Setting. These verses come early in the second major portion of the address delivered in I John 3:11–5:12. (Readers are asked to consult the comments on "setting" and "structure" for the epistle lesson for the Second Sunday of Easter for additional information.) The theme of this section of the address is "we should love one another." More immediately, however, the verses of this week's lesson come from the initial unit of thought in this second section of the epistle, 3:11-24.

Structure. Having stated the theme, "we should love one another," in 3:11, the address offers a negative illustration of how we should not love in 3:12-15. Then, the verses of our lesson offer positive reasoning in relation to the love command in three phases: (1) vv. 16-18 take Christ as the model for love "in truth and action" and argue for the absolute necessity of love taking actual form; (2) vv. 19-22 give assurance to the members of the community that God is more ready and able to forgive us than we are to forgive ourselves; and (3) vv. 23-24 come back to the level of basic command, but now we find a commandment to believe coupled with the command to love, which is repeated here. There is also a word of assurance given, "the Spirit . . . given us."

Significance. Commentators regularly observe how the author of I John writes ambiguous and nearly incomprehensible sentences. They also point to the verses of our lesson as the nadir of the author's clarity. Thus, every attempt to understand and explicate this passage is a challenge.

To begin, the reflection takes Jesus as the example for our love for Christian brothers and sisters. The immediate temptation is to move from the admonition in the text to the general level of love for humankind, but we should notice that the epistle is highly focused, relating only to the immediate community of believers. The author would even exclude those who consider themselves Christians but with whom he has a sharp difference of opinion! This should not lead to an exclusive address today if we recall that the epistle is related to a highly controversial and very painful split in a specific early Christian community.

Furthermore, certain theological assumptions (or, even declarations) in this passage are clear. First, Jesus Christ is offered as the supreme model of what it means to love. Love is unselfish. Love is genuinely related to others. Love has one put others above oneself even to the point that in love one will lay down one's life in behalf of the other(s). Love is more than lip service. Love that is passive is not true love. True love is active. Thus, we have the evidence of the genuineness of love in its actuality—namely, in its accomplishments. True love may be done but left unspoken, but it certainly is not spoken but left undone.

Verses 19-22 are particularly difficult. Whatever they mean, given the thoughts of the complete epistle, they do not advocate a works righteousness; and they do not suggest that if we do not have a guilty conscience, then things are necessarily acceptable to God. Rather, this paragraph seems to say that we can count on God. If we are aware of sin, we can count on God to forgive us; and if we have lived righteously, we can count on God's approval of our lives. Being "from the truth"—namely, taking our directions in life from God—seems to mean we can count on God in all circumstances of life.

The essence of Christian life is summed up in vv. 23-24 as well as anywhere in all the Johannine writings: We are to believe in God's Son, Jesus Christ, and we are to love one another (as he loves us). God's seal on this style of living is the power and the presence of the Spirit. As Christians our lives are invested in God, and God's life is invested in us. We have an existence that is qualitatively distinct, for we live both toward and by the grace of God. The author understands that believers have a holy personal relationship to God, which is the standard and source of living.

The Gospel: *John 10:11-18*

Knowing the Good Shepherd

Setting. At first reading it is not immediately clear how John 10 follows John 9. John 9:1-41 is a highly polished, integrated series of scenes revolving around the healing of a man born blind. In the final scene of that drama, Jesus confronts the Pharisees and declares their blindness (9:39-41). Following this encounter John 10:1-18 offers metaphorical statements (John calls these "figures of speech") and elaborations about shepherding. As readers of the Fourth Gospel we should understand that the Pharisees are still in view. The negative dimension of the remarks in John 10 are a pointed polemic against the opponents engaged in John 9, but the positive dimensions of the text certainly move to a level directed to all believers in all times and places (see v. 16, "I have other sheep that do not belong to this fold"). In this general context we find the verses of our lesson, which form a meditation on the theme, "I am the good shepherd."

Structure. The thought pattern of this "figure of speech" with its interpretive elaboration is quite fluid. While the progression in thought is less than logical, the speech is not a ramble. Rather, in a somewhat spiraling form, the metaphor begins with, comes back to, and ends with the good shepherd laying down his life. Six basic elements compose this reflection: (1) a basic definition of the good shepherd; (2) a statement of the problem with a hired hand; (3) an assertion of the essential characteristic of the good shepherd (qualified by a comparison of the relationship of the Father and the Son); (4) enigmatic, seemingly future-oriented words about the sheep; (5) an explanation of the occasion of the Father's love; and (6) a declaration of the good shepherd's freedom, power, and obedient relationship to the Father.

Significance. This "good shepherd" speech is about divine freedom and power manifested in vulnerability and self-giving in behalf of others. We see the character of God's own freedom and power at work in the life, death, and Resurrection of Jesus Christ, the Good Shepherd who lays down his life freely for the sheep of his flock. Indeed, we find that for the sake of his sheep the Good Shepherd even takes back up the life he freely laid down, so that genuine selflessness for the sake of others is the character of God's full power.

Two qualifications follow, one explicitly from the text and the other in light of it. First, there is a sharp contrast drawn between the Good Shepherd and the hired hand. The hired hand is concerned with self alone, so there is no devotion to or vulnerability on behalf of the flock. Self-interest, above all, is the motivation—bald love of self for self's sake! Second, the text is not glorifying powerlessness, vulnerability, and self-sacrifice for their own sakes! The way the Good Shepherd lived, died, and was raised was determined by his commitment to the well-being of his sheep. Power and freedom are not inherently bad or to be shunned, and vulnerability and selflessness are not inherently good. Full devotion at all costs to God's will for the well-being of others is the point of Christ's self-sacrifice and exaltation. A call to be Christlike is not a call to self-effacement as a necessary good, rather being like Christ means giving the self in service for the well-being of others, no matter the consequences.

Our lesson also articulates a vision of a unified Christianity ("So there will be one flock, one shepherd," v. 16b). The key to unity is found in the flock coming under the single shepherd. Christians are and always have been a diversified lot, and there is nothing in the call of Christ to suggest that we are to become ridiculously uniform in our sheep-ness so that we can be a united flock. True, there is no vision of goats or wolves among the sheep, but the unity of the flock is not founded in the uniformity of the sheep, but in the singleness of the shepherd. It is Christ who unifies an otherwise diversified portion of the human community into the Christian flock. We are brought together by our mutual relationship to the Good Shepherd. His lordship establishes our unity, and we are related to one another, despite real differences, because we are each and every one (individuals and denominations) related to Christ and under his guidance.

One final crucial observation: At the heart of this text is a profound theological truth that is worked out in terms of the concept of "knowing." As believers we have communion with our Lord, Jesus Christ; he knows us and we know him. Prior to this relationship, indeed forming the basis of this relationship, is the mutual knowledge of the Father and the Son. In effect, the text tells us that we know God through our knowledge of and our being known by Jesus Christ. God approaches us in Jesus Christ, and we approach God through the relationship Jesus Christ has established with us.

Easter 4:   The Celebration

The Gospel lesson gives this Sunday the designation of Good Shepherd Sunday. That explains why Psalm 23 is appointed although it has no reference to the preceding lesson from Acts or the one immediately following from I John. John Newton's hymn, "How Sweet the Name of Jesus Sounds," connects both the emphasis on the name in Acts with the Shepherd in John and thus serves as a particularly appropriate hymn for this day. Note that not every hymnal includes the stanza with the shepherd image. It may be found in at least the following: *The Book of Hymns* (United Methodist, 1964), no. 81; *The Hymnal 1982* (Episcopal), no. 644; *The Hymnbook* (Presbyterian, 1955), no. 130; *Hymns for the Family of God* (nondenom., 1976), no. 229; *Lutheran Book of Worship* (1978), no. 345. Both text and tune (St. Peter) are in the public domain.

The Twenty-third Psalm is available in a large number of metrical versions. Most hymnals include at least "The Lord's My Shepherd, I'll Not Want" and "The King of Love My Shepherd Is." The gospel hymn, "He Leadeth Me," is also based on imagery from the psalm.

There are some scriptural texts that draw debate, division, and "party spirit" by their mere utterance, and preachers need to be sensitive to how they will be heard by the congregation and how they may have been heard (and proclaimed) in the past or present in other contexts. Peter's declaration that "there is no other name under heaven given among mortals by which we must be saved" is just such a text. The exclusivity, legalism, and parochialism that such a text might engender might be informed by reasonable exegesis and by thoughtful consideration of Jesus' statement in the Gospel lesson that he has other sheep not of this fold whom he must bring. The power of the name is in the One at whose name every knee shall bow. The Church participates in the power of the name only to the degree that we are in Christ, baptized into his name, and therefore engaged in his ministry of salvation for all. Some paranoid Christians are so apt to draw upon this text for their own ends that pastors have an opportunity to help their flock think responsibly in light of the larger tradition of scriptural interpretation, which emphasizes the breadth of God's love and grace.

Fifth Sunday of Easter

Texts from Acts and Psalms

Acts 8:26-40 is the account of the conversion of the Ethiopian eunuch. Psalm 22:25-31 is a song of praise.

The Lesson: *Acts 8:26-40*

The Ethiopian Eunuch

Setting. The geographical setting of Acts changes after 8:3 from Jerusalem to its surrounding areas. A new character also takes center stage in Acts 8 along with the change of setting. Philip is one of the seven persons chosen to distribute food to the needy in 6:1-6. Acts 8 includes two stories of missionary activity by Philip outside of Jerusalem. The first concerns the conversion of Samaritans and Philip's interaction with Simon the Magician (vv. 4-25), and the second is the conversion of the Ethiopian eunuch, south of Jerusalem in Gaza (vv. 26-40). Some scholars conclude that 8:26-40 shares a number of similarities to the miracle account of Jesus meeting the two disciples on the road to Emmaus in Luke 24. Thus two tasks emerge for interpreting this story: (1) determining what if anything is miraculous about this story and (2) raising the question of why Luke chose to frame the conversion of the Ethiopian eunuch in the context of a miracle story.

Structure. Two different kinds of motifs are present in the structure of Acts 8:26-40. The first is a series of divine directives to Philip: He is commanded to go to Gaza in v. 26, then he is commanded to approach the chariot of the Ethiopian eunuch in v. 29, and finally the spirit whisks Philip away in v. 39. The second structuring device is the series of questions by the Ethiopian eunuch: His initial question is a rhetorical reply to Philip in v. 31, "How can I [understand what I am reading] unless someone guides me?" Then he asks an interpretative question about what he was reading—the suffering servant from Isaiah 53, "About whom, may I ask you, does the prophet say this, about himself or about someone else?" Finally, after a discussion concerning the christological implications of the suffering servant, the eunuch stops the discussion with the words: "Look here is water! What is to prevent me from being baptized?" The interrelationship of imperatives and rhetorical questions is a clue to the meaning of the passage.

Significance. What if anything is miraculous about this story? And, why has Luke chosen to structure this encounter in the genre of a miracle?

Certainly the conversion of the eunuch is not the miracle. Rather the miracle is present in Philip's activity. Frequently a miracle story includes one central divine action like the sudden appearance of Jesus with the disciples on the road to Emmaus, which in this case is followed by his just as sudden departure. The story of Philip and the Ethiopian eunuch is a peculiar miracle story. It shares the sudden departure of the Emmaus story, but it certainly doesn't share the sudden introduction. In fact it takes two very explicit divine commands before Philip finally encounters the Ethiopian eunuch. He is not only directed to the chariot by an angel, but then he must be commanded by the Spirit to approach it once he is there. Then, once Philip does approached the eunuch, he encounters a convert to Judaism that is for all practical purposes already a closet Christian. He just happens to be reading a suffering servant song and wonders whether the passage may be eschatological. At this point in the story Philip finally gets to proclaim the gospel but it is little more than fill-in-the-blanks, prompting the eunuch to request baptism, at which moment Philip disappears.

Luke is suggesting at least two things that are important for preaching this text. First, the spread of the gospel is not dependent on the power of the messengers. The previous story of Philip and Simon the Magician provides an important introduction for this point. In this story Philip is introduced as a wonder worker who could even convert

Simon the Magician. Although Philip is portrayed as being powerful, there remains a subtle contrast in this story between Philip, who proclaimed the kingdom of God, and Simon, who predicated the power of God to himself. The conversion of the Ethiopian eunuch explores this contrast further by subordinating Philip's role in the story to the point where he is almost unnecessary. The message implicit in this structure is very clear: Conversion is clearly the activity of God (both in the sending of Philip and in speaking to the Ethiopian eunuch through Scripture), and it is not the result of human persuasion. Second, the eager acceptance of the gospel by the Ethiopian eunuch underscores its universal claims. These claims are not yet realized with the Ethiopian eunuch for he is presented as a convert to Judaism. They will be realized in the lesson for next week, with the conversion of Cornelius.

The Response: *Psalm 22:25-31*

A Thanksgiving

Setting. Psalm 22 separates into two very different parts. Verses 1-21 are a lament in which the psalmist petitions God for salvation from a great distance. The focus changes to thanksgiving in vv. 22-31 in light of God's response. Psalm 22, therefore, covers the vast range of language in the psalter from despair to joy. The lectionary text picks up the language of thanksgiving in the second half of the psalm.

Structure. It is difficult to break vv. 25-31 into smaller structures. It is worth noting, however, that the second half of the psalm actually begins in v. 22, when the psalmist addresses the congregation in worship with the intent to praise God. The setting of praises, therefore, is firmly anchored in the worshiping community.

Significance. When Psalm 22:25-31 is read in conjunction with Acts 8:26-40, the thanksgiving quite naturally becomes a celebration of the conversion of the Ethiopian eunuch. And this is clearly how it is best used in planning a worship service. The theme that stands out in this context is the universal implication of God's rule (vv. 27-28) and the prediction that this rule will be proclaimed to future generations (vv. 30-31).

New Testament Texts

Further readings from I John and the gospel according to John continue the predominant path taken during the weeks after Easter. The text from the epistle focuses once again on the main topic of the address—that is, love. Here, we find further reflection on the nature and demands of love. The Gospel lesson is still another metaphorical speech by Christ that is primarily christological but which makes strong appeals to believers to live appropriately as disciples of Jesus Christ. While the passages are not necessarily coordinated, they fit together well, forming a complement to each other, because of the distinctive and arcane character of Johannine thought and language.

The Epistle: *I John 4:7-21*

"Because Love Is from God"

Setting. This lesson derives from the second major section of the address of the epistle (3:11–5:12). The theme of "love one another" continues here, and the author adds further nuances to the concept of Christian love throughout the verses of this lesson.

Structure. The train of thought in this lesson is very deliberate. The passage has three parts: First, it begins with the salutation, "Beloved," which is repeated in v. 11. The first "beloved" introduces an injunction ("let us love one another,") which is immediately given a theological basis ("because love is from God") and existential relevance ("everyone who loves is born of God and knows God"). Verse 8 introduces a polemical note and follows that with an affirmation about God. This theological affirmation is developed in v. 9 by means of a concrete example. Verse 10 further specifies the nature of love in both a negative, perhaps polemical, statement and a positive declaration, which is given a concrete basis. Verse 11 brings the injunction and theological reasoning of v. 7 full circle, but now the logic is inverted:

Verse 7	A	Beloved, let us love one another
	B	because love is from God
Verse 11	B	Beloved, since God loved us so much
	A	we also ought to love one another

Second, v. 12 brings a transition in thought. There is continuity with vv. 7-11, but two new ideas are introduced, "abiding" and "love made perfect." Verses 13-16 develop the idea of abiding; vv. 17-18 (and probably 19-20) develop the the notion of "love made perfect." Third, v. 21 is a summary statement and an injunction. This verse exposes the thread that runs through the whole of vv. 7-20—the idea of divinely ordained, mutual love—and offers a succinct statement of the essence of the previous verses (v. 21b).

Significance. Seeing the pattern of logic in these verses goes a long way toward their interpretation and is quite suggestive for preaching on this passage. The sweep of this text is so grand, however, that one may profitably restrict the actual reflection in sermon-building to either vv. 7-11 or 12-20 (21), using the structure of either of those sections for meditation on the theme of love.

Love in the Johannine community appears to be the continuation of the manifestation of the love of God that was first manifested in Jesus. What, then, is the nature of this love? What is the model for this concept of love?

The nature of the love advocated by I John is to be understood in relation to the origin of love with God (v. 19). Love finds its significance in its origin (v. 10), and love's gracious nature determines the results of our receiving that love ourselves (v. 11). The contours of God's love for us (vv. 9-10) are made evident in our acceptance and manifestation of that love (v. 7). According to I John, the nature of love is self-giving and self-effacement in behalf of others, which establish us in confidence in God's presence.

We learn about love through the act of Jesus Christ in laying down his life for us—that is, the manifestation of God's love in Jesus Christ becomes the model for our love. The logic seems to be this: Jesus Christ is the one who abides in God's love, and as a result of this abiding Jesus Christ loves the Christian community. In turn, the believers are to abide in the love of Jesus Christ. Such abiding produces not only a love for God but also love for our brothers and sisters in the faith (v. 21).

In these verses the Christian is consistently admonished to love fellow Christians. Christians are also expressly forbidden to love the world and the things in the world. We see here that love is the dynamism of intramural relations among Christians. The Christian community itself, not the larger world, is understood to be the locus of life that continues and realizes the love of God incarnated in Jesus Christ. This comes as both blessing and responsibility.

The Gospel: *John 15:1-8*

The Vine and the Branches

Setting. We have seen that scholars refer to the second part of the Fourth Gospel (13:1–20:31) as "the book of glory," indicating that the story of Jesus' "hour" that is told here is the story of his glorification in fulfilling God's purposes. The other Gospels have general parallels to this portion of John in their Passion narratives. In John, however, the various scenes and elements of the Passion account are much longer than the comparable materials in the Synoptic Gospels. Chapter 13 recounts Jesus' last meal with his disciples. Chapters 14–17 record Jesus' last discourse and his prayers for his disciples and all believers. Chapters 18–19 tell the story of Jesus' Passion, narrating the events of the Passion from the garden to the grave.

Structure. The thought pattern of this text is somewhat elliptical, although the basic thoughts and ideas are straightforward. The metaphor of the vineyard allows the meditation to move from the vine to the vine dresser to the branches. In turn, the focus of the text moves from the dynamics of the relationship between the vine and the dresser to those between the dresser and the branches to those between the vine and the branches. All along the way the meditation issues a combined threat about fruitlessness and promise about fruitfulness to the branches, and, in turn, the text makes a steady appeal to the branches to "abide" in the vine. The promised fruitfulness of believers accomplished through abiding in Christ is declared to be the glory of God.

Perhaps the sermon should take the tone of an appeal, incorporating elements of promise (and threat—though this should not be overdone given the essentially positive cast of this passage). The structure may be derived from the series of point-of-view shifts inherent in the development of the metaphor: Vine and dresser, dresser and branches, and vine and branches. The "payoff" of the proclamation should relate to the glory of God, so that the sermon does not reduce the message to a mere moral appeal to "bear fruit." We should never lose sight of the notion at the heart of the metaphor of the vine—that is, the vine bears fruit through the branches, not vice versa. The logic is this: Christ is the source of life for the faithful believer, and God is the one who cares for Christ. As the believer lives according to Christ, God is glorified.

Significance. Our lesson is one of many "I am" speeches delivered by Jesus in the Fourth Gospel. The "I am" portion of each of these formulas ("I am the good shepherd," "I am the way, the truth, and the life," "I am the true vine," and so on) makes a play on the well-known "I am" formula from the Old Testament (the divinely stated personal name of God). Recall in Exodus 3 when Moses asked God who he should tell the Israelites sent him, God answered, "I am." The Fourth Gospel meditates frequently on God's name, regularly coupling it with ideas, words, images, or metaphors that give expression to who Jesus Christ is as the Son of God. The verses of our lesson build off the assumption of Jesus' divinity to articulate the nature of his relationship both to God as the Father and to humanity as the lost children of God who Jesus came to redeem and reconcile to God.

Let us state the thought of our lesson in the abstract: The work of mediation in reconciliation is effected in the very person of Jesus himself. On the one hand he relates to God, and on the other he relates to humanity; and as he is related to one and the other, they are indeed related to each other. In this relationship, through Jesus Christ, God cares for humanity and deals with the human condition. Humans experience God's care in both its positive and negative dimensions, for as God works in relation to humanity through Jesus Christ good is nurtured while evil is eliminated.

Within the development of the metaphor of our lesson are several crucial truths. First, Jesus Christ, the living Lord, is the source of whatever good our lives yield in his name to the glory of God. Second, we are called to the gracious experience of investing our lives in Jesus Christ. As we give our lives to him and submit to his lordship, we are promised that our lives will generate results that are in keeping with

God's own will and purposes. Coupled with this promise is a negative word—that is, fruitless discipleship guarantees condemnation. Third, in terms of the metaphor of the vine we are told that unproductive branches will be trimmed and burned. Exactly what this means is not explicit. Indeed the "threat" of being burned is the back side of the promise of fruitfulness for those who are productively invested in Jesus Christ. At a minimum we may conclude (and say) that God works among us in and through Jesus Christ with the expectation that there will be real and discernible results in our lives and in the community of faith in which we live.

The call of the text is to deep, thorough, profound involvement with the work of God through Jesus Christ. We learn that lives transformed into productive, fruitful existence are God's aim and God's glory.

Easter 5: The Celebration

Very little room has been reserved in the gallery of saints for St. Philip, in spite of the amount of coverage he gets from Luke. The Roman Martyrology assigns him the date of June 6, but the Roman Missal ignores him entirely and gives that day to St. Norbert, a German of the eleventh century. Even the Egyptian church, which, according to today's lesson from Acts, ought to be greatly in his debt, pays him scant attention. It may be that he has suffered from a confusion of identities, since he bears the same name as one of the Twelve, and when he gets referred to in Acts 21 as "the evangelist," that has only tended to reinforce an identification with the apostle. The Revised Common Lectionary has, then, rendered us a great service by bringing Philip before us once every three years as a model of what it means to live under the impulse of the Resurrection faith.

Philip's ministry may be used as a case study or illustration of the principles set forth in the other two readings. His activity is under the direction of the Spirit (I John 4) and he leads the Ethiopian to confess Jesus (I John 4) and to seek baptism which incorporates him into the vine and the branches (John 15). All of this is the work of God's love reaching out to the world through those who have already experienced the love of God.

The second stanza of Wesley's hymn "Captain of Israel's Host" is pertinent to references in today's first two lessons. It might be used as a response to the first lesson and a preparation for the second.

> By thine unerring Spirit led,
> We shall not in the desert stray;
> We shall not full direction need,
> Nor miss our providential way;
> As far from danger as from fear,
> While love, almighty love, is near.

This may be sung to St. Catherine ("Faith of Our Fathers") or Melita ("Eternal Father, Strong to Save").

The Acts lesson can provide occasion for including in this Sunday's intercessions prayers for Egypt and its government, the Church in Egypt, catechumens, and the newly baptized. Prayer resources concerning Egypt can be found in *With All God's People: The New Ecumenical Prayer Cycle,* compiled by John Carden (Geneva: WCC, 1989), pp. 4-6.

Sixth Sunday of Easter

Texts from Acts and Psalms

Acts 10:44-48 is the story of the conversion of Cornelius. Psalm 98 is a hymn of praise celebrating the rule of God.

The Lesson: *Acts 10:44-48*

The Gospel for All?

Setting. The lesson is a central episode in the account of the conversion of Cornelius in Acts 10:1–11:18. This story is important to the book of Acts because it underscores the central problem that faced the early Church in its attempt to interpret the gospel. The issue simply put is this: Is the Good News for all people? And if so, what are the implications for proclaiming the gospel? Or to state the problem in contemporary language: How must the gospel be contextualized?

Luke considered the challenge of contextualizing the gospel to be so important for the early Church that the only other story in the book of Acts to receive as much attention as the conversion of Cornelius is the account of Pentecost in Acts 2. In fact, some scholars suggest that the conversion of Cornelius is best interpreted as yet another Pentecost, "that the gift of the Holy Spirit had been poured out even on the Gentiles" (Acts 10:45).

Structure. The first problem in structure is with the present boundaries of the text. These few verses do not make clear the tension and resistance within Peter that is central to this story. In view of this you may want to expand the lesson to include selected verses in Acts 10 that illustrate how the conversion of Cornelius is in many ways also a conversion of Peter. Second, as noted above, the outpouring of the

Holy Spirit in Acts 10:44-48 must be read in conjunction with Pentecost in Acts 2. This relationship will provide our point of entry for interpreting the conversion of Cornelius. .

Significance. The book of Acts begins with the outpouring of the Holy Spirit on the disciples. This marks the inauguration of the Church, and Peter takes on a central role in the event, especially with his sermon (see Acts 2:14-40). Although the seeds of a universal mission are planted in this sermon (Acts 2:9-11, 39), the primary focus is Israel (Acts 2:14, 22, 36). The focus on Israel is maintained throughout the early chapters of Acts so that the gospel first takes root in the larger context of Judaism, which is only natural, since the disciples themselves are religious Jews. As a result the early Church was kosher and law-observant. The conversion of Cornelius is a central story in Acts because it is being used by Luke to force the early Church to come to grips with the limitations of their own ethnicity and cultural context in proclaiming a universal gospel.

Peter plays a primary role in this second Pentecost story, just as he did in the first, but he is not the central character in Acts 10:1–11:18. Notice how Acts 10 begins with Cornelius, who is presented as one who seeks God independently, and how an angel of God directs him to Peter. (This is very similar to the relationship of the Ethiopian eunuch and Philip in the lesson from last week.) The challenge for Peter, when he enters the story, is whether he can recognize the work of God when it does not conform to the cultural context in which he appropriated the gospel. This is no easy matter, and Peter initially fails by not understanding the vision of clean and unclean food. Yet, once Peter is properly instructed by Cornelius, he acquires insight and concludes: "I truly understand that God shows no partiality, but in every nation anyone who fears him and does what is right is acceptable to him" (10:35-36). Peter's ability to see God's salvation even when it did not conform to his own cultural context is so significant that it prompts a second Pentecost even before he could finish speaking (10:44).

If we simply read the account of the conversion of Cornelius in the historical past, then it becomes easy to see the problem, first, of Peter and, then, of the Jerusalem church, which later criticized Peter for eating with uncircumcised people (11:2). How could the Jerusalem church elevate kosher laws to such a degree where these laws became a prerequisite for presenting the gospel to all people? The challenge of peaching this text is to communicate that the conversion of Cornelius is not a story about the shortcomings of Judaism or the irrelevance of kosher laws. Rather it is a story about the importance of contextualizing the gospel, and the need for Christians to see the saving activity of God in cultural contexts that are unfamiliar to us. The problem of contextualizing the gospel is multifaceted. It is not a call to deny our own cultural context for interpreting the gospel but to recognize and to encourage the work of the Spirit in people who are different. A sermon on this text could explore this problem at the level of distinct national and international cultures, but the preacher might also probe the "culture" of a specific congregation. What are its kosher laws? If a local congregation can meet the challenge of contextualizing the gospel, then Luke would say that they, along with Peter, have experienced yet another Pentecost. If they cannot meet this challenge, then they join the circumcision party of the Jerusalem church, whose particular cultural understanding of the gospel became the basis for prejudice.

The Response: *Psalm 98*

A Song of Praise

Setting. Psalm 98 is a song of praise, which incorporates many motifs from the exilic prophet, Second Isaiah. Examples include the call to sing a new song in v. 1 (Isaiah 42:10), and the reference to all people seeing the salvation of God in v. 3 (Isaiah 40:5). The correspondence of motifs has prompted scholars also to interpret Psalm 98 as a celebration of God's second exodus, which for Israel was the return from exile.

Structure. The psalm can be divided between vv. 1-3 and 4-9. The first section celebrates God's new salvation through the imagery of a divine victory. Already in this opening section the new victory of salvation is placed in the larger context of the nations (vv. 2, 3). The second section is a series of summons to praise, that are directed to both the nations and the earth.

Significance. The correspondence between Psalm 98 and Second Isaiah provides insight for using the psalm in worship in conjunction with Acts 10. Most noteworthy is the correspondence between Psalm 98 as a celebration of a second exodus and Acts 10 as the account of a second Pentecost. Both texts probe the universal implications of these actions. This relationship is rich and could be explored both in the construction of a sermon and in the liturgy. Hans-Joachim Kraus provides a point of departure for exploring the interrelationship between Psalm 98 and Acts 10 in his commentary on Psalms.

> Psalm 98 is in all its statements dependent on Deutero-Isaiah. This means that the singer of the psalm takes up the eschatological message. The boarders of the people of God are transcended by the wondrous "second exodus," the end-time salvific act of God. In precisely this basically eschatological event the God of Israel comes to the world. He appears as the king of all creation before the eyes of all nations.

What Kraus states here of God in Psalm 98, could also be said of the second outpouring of the Spirit in Acts 10.

New Testament Texts

Our Easter season lessons move ahead in I John and John's Gospel. Familiar themes are repeated. A congregation that has been wrestling with the New Testament texts over the past weeks may now begin to be at home with the Johannine language and mind, although mere reiteration of the strange language of that early Christian community may remain puzzling or even grow tedious. The preacher must take precautions.

The Epistle: *I John 5:1-6*

Believing in and Living God's Love Through Jesus Christ

Setting. I John 5:1-12 seems to draw together the main themes of the epistle: belief, love, testimony, and life; and these are pondered in relation to God, the Son, the Spirit, and the believers. These twelve verses bring the body of the address to a conclusion by working from the point of view of belief (or faith) through the notions of victorious love, divine testimony, and divine life. The logic unfolds through this concluding section. Our lesson is but part of this larger reflection that

153

evolves in stages: vv. 1-5 treat belief and love; vv. 6-12 ponder testimony and life.

Structure. The thought spirals in the verses of our lesson. In vv. 1-5 we learn that we have our identity as children of God through our belief in Jesus Christ. As believers we live lives characterized by love. Both belief and love are theological categories, since they come from God and relate to God. Yet, the love from God and of God is seen in our love for the community of faith. We love the community in obedience to God's will, and this leads to victory over the world; so that the one victorious over the world is the one who believes that Jesus is the Son of God. A phrase-outline of this spinning thought would be

A. Identity as God's children through belief in Jesus Christ
B. Believers live lives of love
C. Love comes from and moves toward God
D. God commands us to love other believers
E. Through belief in God's Son we have victory over "the world"

It may be that this logic is chiastic, so that rather than A/B/C/D/E one should envision an A/B/C/B/A pattern. If so, the central thought in this reasoning is truly the controlling idea—namely, love comes from and moves toward God. In turn, v. 6 introduces the following section of thought related to testimony. The language is a kind of code that the Johannine community would grasp, but without instruction it can escape even believers today. From the thought of "belief in Jesus Christ" the author thinks of the identity of God's Son from whom flowed the Spirit ("water") because he was glorified in his crucifixion and subsequent death, Resurrection, and exaltation (all of which are summarized as "blood"). To this identity the (Christ-given) Spirit bears witness, and the Spirit is truth—that is, divine reality and verification.

Significance. This text addresses Christians, telling us who we are, what we are to be about, who our Lord is, and how we know it. The language of the passage is esoteric and the line of thought seems contorted. Indeed, even the basic point of view is hard to appreciate, for it is thoroughly theological. The author speaks as if he were standing in the very shoes of God. No mere mortal could know the things declared in these verses, and to that the author would agree wholeheartedly. The elder assumes that the veracity of his own words are rooted in the testimony and illumination of the Spirit. The ability to know, to believe, to obey, and to love are not capacities originating in this world; rather, they are the work and gifts of God.

Because we are born of God, we believe. It is the work of God that has priority and that has established the transformed quality of our lives. As God grasps our lives and enables us to believe in his Son, Jesus Christ, God loves us and enables us to love. Our love is an obedient result of God's own love, and as we live obediently we love others whose lives have been grasped and transformed by the power of God seen in Jesus Christ and still at work through the Spirit. There is no real explanation for what is being said here, and there is not any mechanical proof. The believers know the truth of what I John declares and, because of the work of the Spirit, understands that belief yielding the obedience of love leads to victory.

This text is less didactic and hortatory than edifying. Its bold declarations strike the ears of faith and find a ready hearing. The claims of the text are profound—believers are transformed in their identity and in the quality of their existence; and the implications of the text are enormous—belief in Jesus Christ as the Son of God means an obedient relationship to God that is worked out in the Christian community as a life-style of love. Yet the author does more declaring than unpacking; since he apparently assumes the readers know precisely what he means and what it means for them.

The Gospel: *John 15:9-17*

The Gift and the Demand of God's Abiding Love

Setting. Readers are asked to consult last week's discussion of setting for the Gospel lesson. Our text this week follows immediately after the "I am the true vine" speech by Jesus in John 15. Verse 8 drew on the vineyard metaphor with the mention of fruit, and v. 9 leaves the language of the metaphor while continuing to reflect on the notion of "abiding." Only at v. 16 does the image of fruit come back into play briefly. Thus, our lesson fits its context, but it is not absolutely bound to it or dependent upon it for intelligibility.

Structure. The passage constructs a theological frame of reference by referring to the love of God. In turn, it presents Jesus Christ as the model of Christian life. He abides in God's love and gives himself to and in behalf of others. Thus, the source of Christian love is God's love, and the paradigm of Christian life is Jesus himself.

We find the structure of the lesson in its patterns of relationship among characters and in its statements about the outcome of those associations. Thus we may view the text in terms of the characters: God, Christ, and Christians—with God in full charge and Christians called into a relationship with God through the person and work of Jesus Christ. We may also view the passage in terms of results: Because of the work of Christ, Christians are now friends of God through Christ, and they are able to love one another because the capacity to do so is given them by God.

Significance. The themes of this passage repeat those of previous sections: abiding love, keeping the commandments, the christocentric definition of love, the benefits of Christ, asking in Jesus' name, and divine initiative and power for Christian life. The development of these themes is also repetitive, perhaps reminding us that it is ever necessary to go back over the basics of our faith.

God's own love has been manifested in the selfless sacrificial love of Jesus Christ. The outcome of Jesus Christ's life or love is a call to his disciples to share in this same manner of loving life. Christ is presented here as both the example and the one who empowers his disciples for genuine Christian living. God's own initiative is manifested in the initiative of Jesus as he calls disciples to live in and out of a new relationship to God.

The outcome of what God is doing in Jesus Christ is that believers have a new identity (''friends'') and they are assured that God is still at work manifesting his love in their lives. In this context the commandment to love is more than a regulation or a requirement. It is a promise. The believer is not called to do anything other than what God has done in Jesus Christ and what God wills to do through the lives of the believers. Jesus' words, ''You did not choose me but I chose you,'' are humbling, but more so, they are a comfort; as becomes clear in the following line, "And I appointed you to go and bear fruit, fruit that will last, so that the Father will give you whatever you ask in my name" (v. 16). Commission and promise are two sides of the same coin. The gift and the demand of God's saving grace are the same—that we live lives of godly love by virtue of our relationship to God through his Son, Jesus Christ.

Easter 6: The Celebration

As noted in the commentary, the portion of the lesson from Acts prescribed by the lectionary does not allow for enough understanding of the context. This may be remedied in at least three ways.

One way is to expand the reading itself. Minimally this would require reading vv. 25-26 and 34-35 in addition to 44-48. If such a division of verses is used, it is preferable to have them all printed out in sequence so that the reader can proceed without interruption and not have to jump from place to place in the book.

Another approach is to have the reader do a brief introduction that sets the stage for the reading as we saw three weeks ago. Such an introduction might go as follows:

In today's lesson Cornelius, a Roman centurion, has sent for Peter to come and speak to his household. Up to now the gospel had been preached only to Jews, but Peter has been directed in a vision to go to the home of this Gentile. He proclaims the good news to them, with the following results:
[*a brief pause*]
"While Peter was still speaking . . ."

Yet another approach would be to combine the reading with biblical storytelling. This needs to be done with care and great preparation and with consideration of time restraints, but when these are taken into account it can be an effective teaching device. Biblical storytelling is not the same thing as rote memorization (though it cannot be done without memorization), and it is not a substitute for the liturgical reading of the text, but it has its own place in the teaching and preaching ministry of the Church. Those who wish to explore this

157

aspect of ministry further could contact the Network of Biblical Storytellers, 1810 Harvard Blvd., Dayton, Ohio 45406-4599, or refer to the book by Thomas Boomershine, *Story Journey*. Another helpful series of resources for biblical retelling of stories is edited by Michael E. Williams, *Storyteller's Companion to the Bible*. Four volumes on the Old Testament are in print, with four more to come, plus five volumes on New Testament narratives.

On this particular Sunday, the whole of Acts 10 might be told in story form through either v. 33 or v. 43. At that point the reader would begin with the rest of the chapter as the appointed lesson. The reason for distinguishing between the storytelling mode and the reading of the lesson is to emphasize that the Christian community's identity is derived from the apostolic teaching contained in the book and that the storytelling can have no independent existence apart from its source, the book. Both reader and storyteller must be effective proclaimers in a public setting if they are to complement one another's ministries. There is no reason why one person may not do both jobs, of course. The storytelling may be done in one area of the worship space, and then there may be an intentional movement in the course of the telling to the lectern for the subsequent reading.

Before the reform of the calendar, this day in the Christian year was known as Rogation Sunday, and the following three days were the Rogation Days, a time of asking God's blessing (*rogare,* to ask) on the new crops. In many Protestant denominations this day translated into Rural Life Sunday. The lessons do not lend themselves to that kind of emphasis, but the tradition can remind us to include in today's intercessions prayers for those who work on the land, the land itself, and its fruits.

Psalm 98, as we noted on Easter Day, finds a metrical expression in the hymn "Joy to the World." It is a fitting commentary on the extension of the gospel to the Gentiles as recounted in the story of Cornelius. Two other metrical versions are to be found in *The Presbyterian Hymnal* (1990), nos. 218-19.

Seventh Sunday of Easter

Texts from Acts and Psalms

Acts 1:15-17, 21-26 is a speech by Peter, in which he first interprets the death of Judas and then leads the disciples in picking a replacement. Psalm 1 is a wisdom psalm that contrasts the wicked and the righteous.

The Lesson: *Acts 1:15-17, 21-26*

Judas, the Betrayer

Setting. The traditions about Judas in the Gospels are an important element in the Passion of Jesus. The accounts agree in one central detail—namely, that he is the betrayer. He followed the ministry of Jesus from beginning to end, but, as Luke states in Acts 1:25, "[He] turned aside and went to his own place." The details of how Judas betrayed Jesus and his death differ markedly in the Gospels. In Matthew, for instance, Judas initiates the action. He goes to the Jewish leaders and asks what it would be worth to them if he betrayed Jesus. They suggest thirty pieces of silver. He accepts, follows through on the action, then repents, gives back the money, and finally hangs himself, which prompts the chief priest to buy a field named Akeldama ("Field of Blood") with the blood money (Matthew 26:14-16, 25, 47; 27:3-10). In Luke, Judas is less active. Satan, we are told, entered into Judas, prompting his betrayal for money (Luke 22:1-6, 47-53), and Judas does not enter the story again in the Gospel. Instead Peter recounts his fate in Acts 1:15-26, and it is quite different from Matthew. There is no confrontation with the Jewish leaders, no repentance on the part of Judas, and no death by hanging. Rather,

159

Judas, we are told, bought a field with the blood money he received from betraying Jesus, and somehow he fell in this field, split open his intestines, and died. Hence the name of the field, Akeldama. These striking differences illustrate how the historical details of Judas's fate are being shaped to fit the aims of the different Gospel writers, with the result that Judas functions theologically in the Gospels as an archetype, in order to explore the meaning of betrayal for Christians.

Structure. The lectionary reading has eliminated the central verses of Luke's interpretation of Judas in vv. 18-20, and they should be retained in the lesson. When they are included, Acts 1:15-26 includes three parts: a narrative account of the loss of the apostle Judas (vv. 15-19), an interpretation from Scripture of how such a thing could happen and what should be done in light of this tragedy (v. 20), and a narrative account of how a new apostle, Matthias, was chosen to replace Judas (vv. 21-26).

Significance. Three interrelated points are worthy of attention in preaching this text. They are (1) the meaning of Judas as a betrayer, (2) the contrast that is established between the apostles Judas and Matthias, (3) and the setting of the story as a time in between the Ascension of Jesus and Pentecost.

First, Luke's interpretation of betrayal. Luke does not try to account for the betrayal of Judas psychologically. No deep-seated character flaws in Judas are probed, no real angst over his decision to betray Jesus is developed (as it is in Matthew). Instead his action is examined in a matter-of-fact way on two levels. On one level the betrayal of Judas is really a conflict between God and Satan. The evil that caused the death of Jesus is located in Satan, for it is he who enters into Judas and initiates the events of the Passion (Luke 22:3). Yet, on another level, Luke tells us that it is not Satan at all, but Judas who "turned aside [from his apostolic calling] to go to his own place" (Acts 1:25). These two levels of action indicate that Luke does not really provide a neat, theological answer to the betrayal of Judas (or the problem of evil). Instead he merely lays out all the pieces that contributed to the event: Judas was an apostle, yet he was able to reject his calling for money; the betrayal of Jesus cannot simply be located in humans, for

Satan is much larger and far more powerful than human intention (he was able to enter into Judas). God is also involved in the actions of both Judas and Satan, at least to the extent of providing direction for the Church after the fact of the betrayal.

Second, the last point mentioned above—that God is able to provide direction to the Church in spite of betrayal—is the issue that Luke pursues by not exploring in any more detail the betrayal of Judas, and instead, by moving the narrative ahead to the problem of a replacement for Judas. Matthias, therefore, must be seen as an apostle who provides contrast to Judas. Two criteria are given for this selection: The candidate must be (1) someone who accompanied Jesus through his ministry, and (2) someone who could witness to the Resurrection of Jesus. The contrast between Judas and Matthias is not in the first requirement, but in the second—being a witness to the Resurrection. Judas's betrayal of Jesus took him down a different road, which excluded him from the end of the story of Jesus—a point is vividly made in the closing snapshot of a dead Judas with burst intestines.

Third, the setting of this story is noteworthy. In the larger design of Luke-Acts there is a momentary break in time between the early ministry of Jesus and the ministry of the Church; or, to state it another way, between the Ascension of Jesus (Acts 1:6-11) and the coming of the Holy Spirit (Acts 2). The account of how Judas died and of how the disciples replaced him with Matthias is the story that fills this gap. The placement of this story provides insight into how Luke would have us interpret the betrayal of Judas. On the one hand, the betrayal of Jesus by Judas provides questions that cannot really be answered. The fact that an apostle would attempt to stop the mission of Jesus ruptures momentarily the story line of the early Church, leaving us with unresolved questions. On the other hand, it is the Resurrection of Jesus and not an answer to the problem of evil that pushes the story forward, and it is for this purpose that Matthias must be appointed. As soon as this matter is addressed, the break in time is mended and Pentecost begins. The Church moves on in the power of the Resurrection, rather than in its ability to account for the mysteries of evil.

The Response: *Psalm 1*

Two Ways

Setting. Psalm 1 is a powerful example of didactic poetry in the psalter. Its language is reminiscent of Proverbs. The clear indications of wisdom influence in this psalm, as well as its apparent absence in early numbering systems of the psalms (the Western text of Acts 13:33 quotes Psalm 2 as the actual first Psalm), have prompted scholars to argue that Psalm 1 is meant to function as an introduction to the entire psalter. The heading ''two ways'' arises from the sharp contrast in v. 6 between the ''way of the righteous'' and the ''way of the wicked.''

Structure. The contrast between the righteous and the wicked stated so sharply in v. 6 is central to the structure of the entire psalm. Verses 1-3 describe the way of the righteous, while vv. 4-5 (or 6 if it is not read as a concluding summary) provide contrast by describing the fate of the wicked.

Significance. The psalm provides commentary on the contrast between Judas and Matthias that is central to Luke's construction of Acts 1:15-26. A variety of contrasts are explored in the psalm. Meditation on Torah is the primary characteristic of the righteous person. Torah in v. 2 is being understood in this context as Scripture, but even more, as God's moral structure for the world, which is able to provide meaning to human action for anyone who chooses to enter into it. When viewed in this way the Resurrection of Jesus is part of God's Torah, since it is essential for structuring meaningful human action. The wicked person is one who rejects the structure of God's world. Thus, instead of being firmly grounded in an enduring world order (v. 3), such a person becomes chaff, blown by the wind, and destined to perish (vv. 4, 6). Such is the contrast that Luke has constructed in Acts 1:15-26 between the dead Judas, who went ''to his own place,'' and Matthias, who is chosen to proclaim the resurrection of Jesus.

New Testament Texts

The epistle lesson includes verses from the final section of the body of the letter's address, and the text from the Gospel presents lines from

162

the final portions of the lengthy farewell discourse delivered by Jesus immediately before the Passion narrative is recounted. In both lessons we find Johannine language in motifs and metaphors that entice and baffle the reader.

The Epistle: *I John 5:9-13*

God's Testimony unto Belief and Life

Setting. The verses of this final lesson from I John take us to and through the ending of the body of the epistle's address and include the first verse of the epilogue of the document. The theme of divine testimony continues from last week's reading. The motif of life, divinely given life, is brought forth as the author concludes his address and begins to bring the epistle to a close.

Structure. Verses 9-10 continue the remarks about "testimony" begun in v. 8, bringing in the idea of "belief" in relation to testimony. The topic of testimony is still in view in v. 11, but the author moves in a new direction by introducing the theme of "life" into the discussion of testimony; and indeed the reflection on life takes over to the exclusion of the motif of testimony (v. 12). Finally, v. 13 begins the conclusion of the writing with an explanation of the author's purpose for writing (reminiscent of John 20:30-31). Thus, the observable structure of the lesson is

> I. Divine Testimony
> II. Testimony and Belief
> III. Testimony and Life
> IV. Life and Belief.

This scheme of thought may well provide inspiration for the structure of a sermon on the epistle lesson.

Significance. The supreme witness to Jesus from among the three witnesses named in vv. 7-8—Spirit, water, and blood—is the Spirit sent by the Father to give testimony to his Son, who is himself the Truth. The superiority of the Spirit as a witness is related to the indwelling by the Spirit that believers experience. Human testimony is often persuasive, but it is external; whereas God's divine testimony brought by the indwelling Spirit is internal and, thus, greater. The author is not declaring the superiority of the subjective over the objective; to frame the sense of the passage in those terms is to interpret it inaccurately. The contrast here is between external and internal at one level, but the key to the distinction is that the external testimony is human and the internal is divine. We must be careful in recognizing such distinctions. The temptation is to reduce faith to a level of feelings. We should keep in mind that God's Spirit bearing witness within us may well work against our own natural dispositions and tendencies to move us to commitments and actions that are in fact contrary to our normal constitution.

The outcome of the testimony of the Spirit is that we believe. Belief, however, is not cast as an end in itself. Belief means life. Christian belief is a dynamic reality. It may not be reduced either to affirmation to a set of propositions or to a sheer flurry of activities. Christian belief has focus and form, but it is neither completely fixed nor purely fluid. The reception of divine testimony means both belief in Jesus Christ and the living of a life of Christlike love. We trust Christ so fully and turn to him so completely that our lives are lived in flexible conformity to his own life. His life becomes ours as our lives become his. As we believe we are grasped by God's love so richly shown in Jesus Christ that God's love wells up in our lives and transforms and characterizes our existence.

The mind of the author clusters God, the Son, the Spirit, the believer, divine testimony, divinely inspired belief, and divinely formed life. Together these elements are a vital whole that issues in "eternal life." The idea of eternal life has about it both the notions of temporal (everlasting) and qualitative (abundance) superiority in comparison with natural life. The use of this phrase in I John reveals that the qualitative aspect is foremost in the author's mind. Indeed, it is clear that eternal life is not simply futuristic, for it is the present possession—or better, the quality of existence—of those who believe in Jesus Christ. This does not mean there is no future dimension to eternal life—in the mind of the author it clearly continues beyond death, but the chief concern is to present the importance of eternal life as a transformed human existence in the present rather than to develop teaching about life after death.

Eternal life is the life of God. Jesus accomplished the giving of eternal life to believing humans by giving himself in death, so that raised to life, having conquered death, he can communicate eternal life by breathing forth the life-giving Spirit upon them.

The Gospel: *John 17:6-19*

The Security of Knowing Christ's Prayer for Us

Setting. Toward the end of the farewell discourse (John 13–17) Jesus utters a pointed prayer (17:1-26), often referred to as his "High Priestly Prayer" because of the intercessory quality of the petition. Our lesson comes from the heart of that prayer.

Structure. Outlining a prayer is not like outlining a syllogism. Johannine speech is normally difficult, and in the mode of prayer, the logic is challenging because it makes assumptions. Fortunately, in these verses Jesus even pauses to explain himself so that his words are not impossible. The prayer works with three basic ideas. First, Jesus' disciples are God's own persons who have kept God's word and whom God gave to Jesus; the result of this arrangement is that God's people believe Jesus is from God. Thus, we have God, Jesus, and God's people as Jesus' disciples in a triangular relationship. Second, the pattern of the relationship is about to change because Jesus is about to return to his heavenly Father. Thus, Jesus prays for the continued well-being of these believers. Third, the result of Jesus' departure from earth and return to heaven is that he sends forth those who believe in him in the same way that God sent him forth into the world. Thus, the prayer addresses the basic relationship between God, Jesus, and believers, and it reflects upon the forthcoming changes in time, relationships, and the activity of the believers.

Significance. The nature of this prayer suggests the tone of prayerful meditation for proclamation in relation to this text. The content of these verses expresses concern for active disciples, so that the meditation should address the lives of actual believers.

The prayer recognizes the active hand of God in several areas—in the saving work of Jesus Christ, in the granting of discipleship to believers, and in the disciples' being sustained in the world. The main concern of the prayer is the well-being of the disciples after the death and Resurrection of Jesus. All other elements here come into play in relation to that issue. What does the prayer tell us about the life of discipleship?

The prayer is a bold word of assurance. At one level it informs us that we are related to God and Christ because of the active will of God. The call to discipleship is of divine origin, and so we are not saddled with the responsibility of manufacturing our calling. More important, however, is the good news that as disciples we have the privilege of knowing God's truth in Jesus Christ. Our belief, because of God's work, is the very glory of Christ who is himself the very glory of God. God has an investment in our belief, and that implies deep divine concern.

Thus, Jesus prays for the sanctification and consecration of believers—that is, that they grow increasingly in godliness and in devotion to God. This growth is itself cast as the result of God's working in our lives, so again we learn of the benefits of God's love made known—or better—made real in Jesus Christ. Our security in a difficult, even hostile world is found in God's constant care and concern for us in and through Jesus Christ.

The prayer is not a promise that we will face no hardship or perils, rather the opposite seems implied. Jesus prays because of the reality of evil and because of the predictable opposition we shall face as we believe and live in his name. The declaration that Jesus sends believers in the same way that God sent him is practically a promise of persecution, but our security is the same as was Jesus', the love and the power of God.

Easter 7: The Celebration

The story of the election of Matthias testifies to the importance placed by the early Church on the apostolic college as a symbol of the twelve tribes of Israel and of the necessity of the Twelve to guarantee continuity between the Israel of the old covenant and the Israel of the new covenant, the Church. The Twelve were unique, as the qualifications for Matthias indicate, as they were those who could be described as having been with Jesus from the beginning and were witnesses to the Resurrection. The Twelve were understood to be those from whom all subsequent Christian preaching would spring because they were the source of the tradition "about all that Jesus did and taught from the beginning until the day that he was taken up to heaven, after giving instructions through the Holy Spirit to the apostles whom he had chosen" (Acts 1:1-2). This is to say that the Gospel is rooted in a historical event and has its basis in events rather than speculative philosophy. The Twelve symbolize the historical roots of the faith. Today's narrative about Matthias, coming at the point between the celebration of the Ascension this past Thursday and the Pentecostal anointing of the Spirit that is celebrated next week, is a reminder that although the Church is dependent upon the Spirit for its ongoing life, it lives in fidelity to the apostolic testimony and is not subject to "every wind of doctrine." The Spirit operates once the stage for the drama of salvation has been set in history (see commentary above). A theme that emerges here is the balance between tradition and change as the Church seeks to be faithful to its commission. It is necessary to have the Twelve, it seems; it is not important that one of them be Judas.

The coupling of the election of Matthias with the high priestly prayer provides an opportunity to examine the use of *sanctify* and *send* as they apply to Christian vocation. Christ is offering himself in John 17, but it is clear that the Church is also being offered to God. Matthias is one of those who has been guarded (John 17:12) and not been lost. Christians are sanctified and sent into the world, shielded by Christ, to do his work in the world. The election of Matthias is a sign that God's will is not defeated. An early Christian writer, in a work called The Letter to Diognetus, seems almost to be commenting on today's Gospel lesson:

What the soul is in the body, that Christians are in the world. The soul is dispersed through all the members of the body, and Christians are scattered through all the cities of the world. The soul dwells in the body, but does not belong to the body, and Christians dwell in the world, but do not belong to the world. . . . The flesh hates the soul and treats it as an enemy, even though it has suffered no wrong, because it is prevented from enjoying its pleasures; so too the world hates Christians, even though it suffers no wrong at their hands, because they range themselves against its pleasures. The soul loves the flesh that hates it; in the same way, Christians love those who hate them. The soul is shut up in the body, and yet itself holds the body together; while Christians are restrained in the world as in a prison, and yet themselves hold the world together. . . . It is to no less a post than this that God has ordered them, and they must not try to evade it. (Cyril C. Richardson, ed., *Early Christian Fathers,* The Library of Christian Classics, vol. 1 [Philadelphia: Westminster, 1953], p. 218)

Pentecost

Old Testament Lessons

Ezekiel 37:1-14 is the eerie story of the dried and windblown bones that spring back into life as though we were watching a movie backwards. Psalm 104:24-34, 35*b* is a hymn celebrating the creative power of God.

The Lesson: *Ezekiel 37:1-14*

Can Bones Be Brought Back to Life?

Setting. The primary setting of the book of Ezekiel is the Exile. The prophetic oracles and visions in the book are addressed to a displaced people, who have lost their land; livelihood; national identity; and, most seriously of all, their faith. Their God, after all, had promised them life in the land as the fulfillment of the Exodus salvation. In exile they now find themselves to be a wilderness people. Unlike the first generation in the wilderness, the exiles are not on the move to a promised land, but just the reverse. Their experience is that they are moving away from the land. It is as though they are leftover characters in a movie where the main drama has already been played out. The exiles are hopeless antiheroes. Ezekiel 1–32 presents judgment oracles against Israel and the nations in an attempt to explain how such a hopeless situation could have come about. Ezekiel 33–48 takes up the more difficult task of raising the question of whether the situation is in fact hopeless. The question that provides the overarching problem for the latter section of the book is stated by the exiles in Ezekiel 33:10, "How then can we live?" The story of the dry bones is an important part of God's answer.

169

Structure. Ezekiel 37:1-14 can be outlined in four sections.

    I. The Setting of the Wilderness and Dry Bones (vv. 1-2)
    II. The Opening Question of God to the Prophet (v. 3)
    III. The Power of the Divine Word (vv. 4-10)
        A. To the bones (vv. 4-8)
        B. To the Spirit (vv. 9-10)
    IV. The Interpretation of the Bones and God's Answer to the
         Opening Question (vv. 11-14)

Significance. The setting is important for an interpretation of the story. Outside of the promised land Israel is a dead people—not because they have lost national identity, but because they are cut off from God, whose presence is tied to Jerusalem and by extension to the land (see the discussion Year A, First Sunday in Advent). In view of this reality, the answer to the question noted above, "How then can we live?" is that exiles cannot live. The opening question to the prophet in v. 3 and the prophet's evasive response simply confirm this answer. When God asks the prophet whether dried bones can be brought back to life, note how the prophet never answers, and, instead, defers the question back to God. The equivocal answer of the prophet goes to the heart of this text. From the prophet's perspective the "You know" response is easily interpreted as an attempt to avoid the obvious—Of course dried bones cannot come back to life. Yet by attempting to avoid the obvious, the prophet does indeed place the answer to the question where it should be and that is with God rather than ourselves. The remainder of the story is God's surprising answer to the question.

Verses 4-10 present a two-part drama to demonstrate the power of the divine word. First, the prophet is commanded to preach to the bones. The power of this word inaugurates the miracle of God reversing time before the eyes of the prophet. The windblown bones are activated, and then muscle, skin and flesh fill out the skeletons. The imagery here is so graphic that it is the section of the story that most of us recall first. But this is not yet the final point of the story, for note how this episode concludes in v. 8 with the prophet telling us that there is no life. The conclusion suggests that God's bending or even reversing of time itself isn't enough.

Life requires the Spirit of God, which becomes the object of the second divine command to the prophet in vv. 9-10. The Spirit of the Lord is a central motif in the story, occurring no less than ten times in fourteen verses. God tells the prophet in vv. 5, 6, 9, 10, 14 that it is the Spirit that gives life. The miracle of this story is not simply that God can reverse time, but that the Spirit of God can give the people life even in the wilderness. Exilic Israel did not think that this was possible for they thought that God was tied to the Jerusalem Temple and the land. God's two-part miracle is an answer to the assumptions of exilic Israelites, who are quoted in v. 11 as saying, "Our bones are dried up, and our hope is lost; we are clean cut off."

The point of the story is that God has left the land to be with his people in the wilderness of the exile. The result of God's surprising decision is that it allows the movie of the exile to be reversed. No longer are these people antiheroes who are moving away from the land and from the presence of God. Rather with God leaving the land in order to journey with Israel, the people once again acquire direction and hope because God is now able to lead them back to the promised land of rest. For the prophet Ezekiel this is no less than a resurrection story. In preaching this text it may be helpful to explore situations or persons in your community where there is consensus that all hope is gone. The power of this text is that it is a bold statement that God is able to reverse such situations—to play them backwards—and to breathe new life into the characters.

The Response: *Psalm 104:24-34, 35b*

Celebrating God's Creative Power

Setting. Psalm 104 is a hymn celebrating the creative power of God. As such it shows a connection to Genesis 1 in vv. 6 and 25 as well as to creation motifs from other cultures in the Ancient Near East. Verses 19-24 have a marked resemblance to the Egyptian hymn of Akhenaton (Amenophis IV), especially with the encyclopedic listing of aspects of creation. In addition, references to primeval waters in vv. 6 and 26 also suggest the influence of a Syro-Canaanite primeval flood mythology.

Structure. The lectionary reading included only the latter portion of Psalm 104. Two problems in structure arise with the given text. First, we should question whether v. 24 is an introduction to what follows, as the lectionary reading would indicate, or a summary to the preceding section of vv. 19-24. Second, the invective against evil in v. 35*a* has been deleted. The invective in v. 35 pulls the psalmist's meditation on creation back into the moral sphere, which is absent if the reading ends at v. 34, or moves too quickly to the doxology in 35*b*. With these two problems as background, the lectionary text can be outlined as follows:

I. Praise of God as Creator (vv. 24-30)
   A. Work (v. 24)
   B. Leviathan (vv. 25-26)
   C. Summary (vv. 27-30)
II. Concluding Praise (vv. 31-34)
   A. Call for continued theophany (vv. 31-32)
   B. Promise to praise (vv. 33-34)
   C. Invective (35*a*)
   D. Doxology (35*b*)

Significance. When Psalm 104 is read in conjunction with Ezekiel 37, the summary statement of God's creative power in vv. 27-30 stands out, for it also employs imagery of the Spirit of God. These verses underscore how the creative power of God is an ongoing process that requires the continual attention of God. The use of the technical word "to create" (Hebrew, *bara'*, also used in Genesis 1) underscores how such ongoing attention to created life is just as powerful as God's original acts of creation. And, as with the moral choices evident in God's pristine world (Genesis 1–3), we also underscore how the moral life requires ongoing attention, lest we be consumed by the earth that God has given us (v. 35*a*).

New Testament Texts

The texts form complements to each other, though they come from different streams of tradition and thought in early Christianity. There are differences of perspective and emphasis, however. Acts narrates the events of Pentecost, whereas the text from John is part of Christ's farewell discourse (John 13–17), wherein he speaks in promising prophetic tones about the forthcoming gift of the Spirit that he, as the yet-to-be crucified, resurrected, and exalted Son of God, will send to his disciples. The difference between these texts may be expressed as the difference between two prepositions. Acts regards the Holy Spirit as coming "upon" the disciples; John understands that the Holy Spirit comes "to" them.

The Epistle: *Acts 2:1-21*

Knowing God's Presence and Having the Courage to Name It

Setting. It is important to notice the setting of the entire Pentecost story in the overall structure of Acts. In Acts 1 we moved from Easter up to Pentecost, seeing the risen Lord present among the disciples, instructing them and promising the coming of the Holy Spirit. Acts 2 narrates the fulfillment of Jesus' promise, and it shows us quite dramatically what the disciples do as a result of being anointed with the Spirit—they are transformed from being mere eyewitnesses to being genuine ministers of the word. The remainder of Acts, beginning in Acts 3, tells how certain faithful disciples continue the Christ-ordained and Spirit-empowered and Spirit-directed mission.

Structure. There are three distinct sections in this lesson: vv. 1-13, vv. 14-16, vv. 17-21. Verses 1-13 have three subsections that provide a narrative introduction to Peter's speech in vv. 14-40. First, we learn of the time and place (v. 1) and, second, vv. 2-4 tell dramatically of the coming of the Holy Spirit upon the disciples. Third, vv. 5-13 introduce and describe the assembly of "devout Jews from every nation" and tell of the mixed reaction of the crowd to the disciples. Verses 14-16 fix the speech in relation to Jerusalem; Pentecost; the cosmopolitan crowd; and, then, make statements about the divine anointing of believers, the ensuing miracle(s), and the misunderstanding of the masses. Verses 17-21 correlate the events of Pentecost with scriptural texts that are interpreted as a prophetic forecast of the incidents Acts recounts.

Significance. Peter's claim is that prophecy is fulfilled in the Pentecost happenings; he identifies divine activity and the presence of the Holy Spirit with the effects on the believers. This allows him to name the time as "the Last Days." In turn, this naming of the time indicates the crucial nature of the Pentecost event as a moment of cosmic crisis and divine judgment. The outcome of the eschatological fulfillment of prophecy at Pentecost is the driving of humanity to call on the name of the Lord in order to be saved.

Notice the boldness of Peter's speech at Pentecost. He made several points clear in this speech, and at least two prominent points are inherent in this week's lesson. First, only those in a positive relationship to Jesus Christ—as the one in whom God's plan was/is fulfilled—are in a position to understand properly the present work of God. The masses could not comprehend the effects of the Holy Spirit on the believers because they had no knowledge of the promise of the risen Jesus that the Spirit would come upon the disciples. The superior knowledge of the disciples is not a source of privilege, but a call to service in behalf of Christ to the masses. Christianity is not gnosticism. Whatever we know by the grace of God is given to us in order to direct us to ministry.

Second, Christians have a peculiar and particular perspective on time: It is the Last Days—a penultimate time of fulfillment, judgment, and salvation. An important dimension of the ministry to which we are called is the naming of the times. Time from the Christian point of view is not a spiral or a circle or even a mere line. Time belongs to God, who changed the time in the life, death, Resurrection, and Ascension of Jesus Christ and the subsequent outpouring of the Holy Spirit. The time of God's promise has been brought to fulfillment. In the current moment, described in the lesson as "the last days," we live under the plain claim of God. The declaration of Peter means that the time for which humanity had hoped had, in fact, already broken into history, so that things were no longer the same. Furthermore, as there is a difference between the time of God's present and the time of the past, brought about by the activity of God, there will be a difference between the present and God's future. We do not simply wait on God, for God in Christ and the Spirit has come in a real, significant way; but God's coming is not fully present and will not be until "the last day." In the present we are called to name God's presence, to change our lives through the power of the Spirit so that they are given in obedience to God's active will, and to look forward confidently and courageously to God's future even amidst less than perfect circumstances.

The Gospel: *John 15:26-27; 16:4b-15*

The Coming of the Truth-Telling Spirit

Setting. Readers are asked to refer to the discussion of setting for the Gospel lessons for the past two weeks. In the verses of this lesson Jesus continues to deliver his farewell discourse, but now the focus moves from (not away from!) Christology to teaching about the coming of the Spirit ("the Advocate").

Structure. The lesson contains three sweeping movements. First, 15:26-27 has Jesus bring up the coming of the Spirit and the activity of the Spirit in testifying to the truth. Second, 16:4b-11 discloses two further crucial activities of the Spirit: (a) comforting the disciples after the death, Resurrection, and exaltation of Jesus; (b) reproving the world with regard to sin, righteousness, and judgment. Third, 16:12-15 promises that with the coming of the Spirit the disciples will experience continuing and increasing illumination concerning the divine.

Significance. The sad fact is that most Christians know and teach precious little about the Holy Spirit. Consult the Apostles' Creed and the Nicene Creed (and the others that are available) and see what we are prepared to confess together as a community of faith about the Holy Spirit. Little indeed, considering the immense importance of the subject. Fortunately this lesson from Jesus' good-bye speech in John is a small gold mine of helpful information about the Holy Spirit. With the materials of these verses in hand we may get an idea of who the Holy Spirit is and what we might expect the Holy Spirit to do among us as members of the Church today. Use of this text for preaching can profitably take a didactic tone (though not condescending!).

We learn that the Spirit is an "Advocate." The Greek word is sometimes translated in near transliteration as "Paraclete." Inherent in this term (or title) is a fairly full statement of the nature and work of the Spirit. In antiquity a "paraclete" was a "mediator," a "comforter," and a "counselor." In other works, a paraclete was one who instructed, assisted, and entered pleas on behalf of someone else. The image of the Spirit as Comforter has been misunderstood throughout history. The comfort provided by a paraclete was the comfort of sound advice and direction, not mere condolence. We do not get the Holy Spirit as a consolation prize because we have suffered the loss of Jesus. Christ's words in this lesson tell us that the coming of the Spirit brings us an advantage previously unavailable (16:7). The question is this, What is the advantage of the presence of the Holy Spirit?

Our lesson gives an answer. The Holy Spirit who is "the Spirit of Truth," is the one who gives convincing testimony on behalf of Jesus Christ. Remarkably, the Spirit does this work of testifying through the disciples of Christ. The power of God works as the Spirit operates through the real lives of believers to bear witness—in word and deed—to the person and work of Christ. Good news: the job of convincing others of the truth of the gospel is not ours at all. We are the agents of the power of the Spirit, but our level of responsibility is not final! The real work of Christian testimony is the task of the Holy Spirit.

The coming of the Spirit brings "comfort" to the disciples of Jesus Christ. Remember, this comfort is not merely emotional; it is factual and actual. On the one hand, there is a negative dimension to this work of the Spirit. "The world" (Johannine code for those outside the Church who do not believe in Jesus Christ) will be shown the error of its ways. The text makes this explicit in terms of three theological issues: sin, righteousness, and judgment. Sin is equated with not believing in Jesus Christ. Righteousness is associated with the crucified and risen Christ being exalted into the presence of the Father, a clear demonstration of his identity and the authenticity of his teaching. And judgment is explicated in terms of the ruler of this world having been condemned. Thus, the work of reproving the world is the work of making known God's truth: Jesus is God's Son; Jesus has been raised and glorified; and Satan and the forces of evil have been ultimately defeated by the work of God in Jesus Christ.

On the other hand, there is a striking positive dimension to the work of the Holy Spirit. (Actually the negative work is positive enough!) The Spirit is God's power at work continuing and increasing the understanding of believers. As the Spirit works, believers have an ever deepening comprehension of Jesus Christ. In turn, a deeper understanding, a deeper appreciation, and a deeper relationship with Jesus Christ—through the work of the Spirit—means deeper perception, thankfulness, and intimacy with God.

Pentecost: The Celebration

The move from white paraments to red and the use of an Old Testament lesson again can give this day the feel of a new season rather than that of a triumphal conclusion to the Great Fifty Days. This is not altogether inappropriate, however, and one can easily understand how for centuries in the Church's practice the Day of Pentecost was thought of as the beginning of a new season. It is understandable because the theme of Pentecost is the new creation, the new thing that God is doing in the world. Yet this new creation is inextricably tied to the Easter event, as is made clear by today's Gospel lesson and the repetition of the Ezekiel lesson from the Easter Vigil. The work of the Holy Spirit that we are celebrating is the continuation of the ministry of Christ. Without that connection we are apt to lose our Trinitarian balance and fall over into a kind of vague Spirit-worship. This connection with the work of Christ is also a corrective against statements like, "Pentecost is the coming of the Spirit into the world," as though the Holy Spirit had not been there from the beginning. Pentecost is the celebration of a specific work of the Spirit, which is the empowerment of the Church for Christ's service in the world.

It is for this reason that the Holy Spirit is called upon by the Church when we intend to perform some serious work. At ordinations we sing the *Veni, Creator Spiritus*. The Great Thanksgiving at the Eucharist, the Thanksgiving over the Water at baptism, and the ordination prayers all have sections known as the epiclesis, a portion of the prayer where God is asked to grant the work of the Holy Spirit in effecting our requests.

177

If the Eucharist is celebrated today, the following epiclesis might be sung by the congregation immediately following the minister's said epiclesis in the Great Thanksgiving. The text is by Charles Wesley and should be sung to an appropriately vigorous tune such as Azmon.

> Come, Holy Ghost, thine influence shed,
>   And [real make] the sign;
> Thy life infuse into the bread,
>   Thy power into the wine.
>
> Effectual let the tokens prove
>   And made, by heavenly art,
> Fit channels to convey thy love
>   To every faithful heart.

In congregations which do not use the Great Thanksgiving, this will serve equally well as the hymn that introduces the Lord's Supper portion of the service.

In some traditions Pentecost has been known as Whitsunday, recalling the custom of performing baptisms on this day when the baptizands would have been robed in white, hence "White-Sunday." Administration of baptism on Pentecost helps remind us both of its connection to Easter and that all baptism is in some way Spirit-baptism. Where baptism is separated from confirmation, Pentecost is frequently the time for confirmation, since it is an act in which the Church requests the strengthening power of the Holy Spirit in the lives of those being confirmed. The new formula at the laying on of hands in *The Book of Common Prayer* is, "Strengthen, O Lord, your servant N. with your Holy Spirit; empower him for your service; and sustain him all the days of his life" (p. 418). Baptisms on Easter Day and confirmations on Pentecost again serve to unify the season and the actions as part of one event through time.

The custom of asking everyone to wear something red to the service and/or to have red helium filled balloons floating above the heads of the congregation is not new in terms of trying to emphasize the day in special ways. Bishop Durandus reported in the early thirteenth century of churches where a dove would be let down into the church from the roof, or where masses of rose leaves and even sparks of fire would be blown out over the congregation!

Scripture Index

Old Testament

179

A Comparison of Major Lectionaries

YEAR B: ASH WEDNESDAY THROUGH THE DAY OF PENTECOST

	Old Testament	Psalm	Epistle	Gospel
ASH WEDNESDAY				
RCL	Joel 2:1-2, 12-17	51:1-17	II Cor. 5:20b–6:10	Matt. 6:1-6, 16-21
RoCath	Joel 2:12-18	51:3-6, 12-14, 16-18	II Cor. 5:20–6:2	Matt. 6:1-6, 17
Episcopal		103		
Lutheran	Joel 2:12-19	51:1-13	II Cor. 5:20b–6:2	
FIRST SUNDAY IN LENT				
RCL	Gen. 9:8-17	25:1-10	I Pet. 3:18-22	Mark 1:9-15
RoCath	Gen. 9:8-15	25:4-9		Mark 1:12-15
Episcopal		25	Mark 1:9-13	
Lutheran	Gen. 22:1-18	6	Rom. 8:31-39	Mark 1:12-15

	Old Testament	Psalm	Epistle	Gospel
SECOND SUNDAY IN LENT				
RCL	Gen. 17:1-7, 15-16	22:23-31	Rom. 4:13-25	Mark 8:31-38
RoCath	Gen. 22:1-2, 9-13, 15-18	116:10, 15-19	Rom. 8:31-34	Mark 9:2-10
Episcopal	Gen. 22:1-14	16		
Lutheran	Gen. 28:10-22	115:1, 9-18	Rom. 5:1-11	Rom. 8:31-39
THIRD SUNDAY IN LENT				
RCL	Exod. 20:1-17	19	I Cor. 1:18-25	John 2:13-22
RoCath		19:8-11	I Cor. 1:22-25	John 2:13-25
Episcopal		19:7-14	Rom. 7:13-25	
Lutheran		19:7-14	I Cor. 1:22-25	
FOURTH SUNDAY IN LENT				
RCL	Num. 21:4-9	107:1-3, 17-22	Ephes. 2:1-10	John 3:14-21
RoCath	II Chron. 36:14-17, 19-23	137:1-6		Ephes. 2:4-10
Episcopal	II Chron. 36:14-23	122	Ephes. 2:4-10	John 6:4-15
Lutheran		27		Ephes. 2:4-10

	Old Testament	Psalm	Epistle	Gospel
FIFTH SUNDAY IN LENT				
RCL	Jer. 31:31-34	51:1-12	Heb. 5:5-10	John 12:20-33
RoCath		51:3-4, 12-15	Heb. 5:7-9	
Episcopal		51		
Lutheran		51:11-16	Heb. 5:7-9	
SIXTH SUNDAY IN LENT (PASSION/PALM SUNDAY)				
RCL	Isa. 50:4-9a	31:9-16	Phil. 2:5-11	Mark 14–15
RoCath		Isa. 50:4-7	22:8-9, 17-20, 23-24	Phil. 2:6-11
Episcopal	Isa. 45:21-25	22:1-21	Mark 14:32-14:47	
Lutheran	Zech. 9:9-10	31:1-5, 9-16		
GOOD FRIDAY				
RCL	Isa. 52:13–53:12	22	Heb. 10:16-25	John 18–19
RoCath		31:2, 6, 12-13, 15-17, 25	Heb. 4:14-16; 5:7-9	
Episcopal		22:1-21	Heb. 10:1-25	John 18:1-19:37
Lutheran		22:1-23	Heb. 4:14-16; 5:7-9	

	Old Testament	Psalm	Epistle	Gospel
EASTER DAY				
RCL	Isa. 25:6-9	118:1-2, 14-24	I Cor. 15:1-11	John 20:1-18
RoCath	Acts 10:34, 37-43	118:1-2, 16-17	Col. 3:1-4	John 20:1-9
Episcopal		118:14-29		Mark 16:1-8
Lutheran		118:1-2, 15-24	I Cor. 15:19-28	
SECOND SUNDAY OF EASTER				
RCL	Acts 4:32-35	133	I John 1:1–2:2	John 20:19-31
RoCath		118:2-4, 13-15, 22-24	I John 5:1-6	
Episcopal	Acts 3:12a, 13-15, 17-26	111	I John 5:1-6	
Lutheran	Acts 3:13-15, 17-26	148	I John 5:1-6	
THIRD SUNDAY OF EASTER				
RCL	Acts 3:12-19	4	I John 3:1-7	Luke 24:36b-48
Ro Cath	Acts 3:13-15, 17-19	4:2, 4, 7-9	I John 2:1-5	Luke 24:35-48
Episcopal	Acts 4:5-12	98	I John 1:1–2:2	
Lutheran	Acts 4:8-12	139:1-11	I John 1:1–2:2	Luke 24:36-49

	Old Testament	Psalm	Epistle	Gospel
FOURTH SUNDAY OF EASTER				
RCL	Acts 4:5-12	23	I John 3:16-24	John 10:11-18
RoCath	Acts 4:8-12	118:1, 8-9, 21-23, 26, 29	I John 3:1-2	
Episcopal	Acts 4:23-37		I John 3:1-8	John 10:11-16
Lutheran	Acts 4:23-33			I John 3:1-2
FIFTH SUNDAY OF EASTER				
RCL	Acts 8:26-40	22:25-31	I John 4:7-21	John 15:1-8
RoCath	Acts 9:26-31	22:26-28, 30-32	I John 3:18-24	
Episcopal		66:1-11	John 14:15-21	
Lutheran		22:24-30	I John 3:18-24	
SIXTH SUNDAY OF EASTER				
RCL	Acts 10:44-48	98	I John 5:1-6	John 15:9-17
RoCath	Acts 10:25-26, 34-35, 44-48	98:1-4	I John 4:7-10	
Episcopal	Acts 11:19-30	33	I John 4:7-21	
Lutheran	Acts 11:19-30		I John 4:1-11	

SEVENTH SUNDAY OF EASTER

	Old Testament	Psalm	Epistle	Gospel
RCL	Acts 1:15-17, 21-26	1	I John 5:9-13	John 17:6-19
RoCath	Acts 1:15-17, 20-26	103:1-2, 11-12, 19-20	I John 4:11-16	John 17:11-19
Episcopal	Acts 1:15-26	68:1-20	I John 5:9-15	John 17:11*b*-19
Lutheran	Acts 1:15-26	47	I John 4:13-21	John 17:11*b*-19

DAY OF PENTECOST

	Old Testament	Psalm	Epistle	Gospel
RCL	Ezek. 37:1-14	104:24-34, 35*b*	Acts 2:1-21	John 15:26-27; 16:4*b*-15
RoCath	Acts 2:1-12	104:1, 24, 29-31, 34	I Cor. 12:3-7, 12-13	John 20:19-23
Episcopal	Acts 2:1-11	104:25-37	I Cor. 12:4-13	John 20:19-23
Lutheran		104:25-34		John 7:37-39*a*

A Liturgical Calendar

Ash Wednesday Through
The Day of Pentecost 1993–2001

	1993 A	1994 B	1995 C	1996 A	1997 B
Ash Wed.	Feb. 24	Feb. 16	Mar. 1	Feb. 21	Feb. 12
Lent 1	Feb. 28	Feb. 20	Mar. 5	Feb. 25	Feb. 16
Lent 2	Mar. 7	Feb. 27	Mar. 12	Mar. 3	Feb. 23
Lent 3	Mar. 14	Mar. 6	Mar. 19	Mar. 10	Mar. 2
Lent 4	Mar. 21	Mar. 13	Mar. 26	Mar. 17	Mar. 9
Lent 5	Mar. 28	Mar. 20	Apr. 2	Mar. 24	Mar. 16
Passion Sun.	Apr. 4	Mar. 27	Apr. 9	Mar. 31	Mar. 23
Holy Thur.	Apr. 8	Mar. 31	Apr. 13	Apr. 4	Mar. 27
Good Fri.	Apr. 9	Apr. 1	Apr. 14	Apr. 5	Mar. 28
Easter Day	Apr. 11	Apr. 3	Apr. 16	Apr. 7	Mar. 30
Easter 2	Apr. 18	Apr. 10	Apr. 23	Apr. 14	Apr. 6
Easter 3	Apr. 25	Apr. 17	Apr. 30	Apr. 21	Apr. 13
Easter 4	May 2	Apr. 24	May 7	Apr. 28	Apr. 20
Easter 5	May 9	May 1	May 14	May 5	Apr. 27
Easter 6	May 16	May 8	May 21	May 12	May 4
Ascension Day	May 20	May 12	May 25	May 16	May 8
Easter 7	May 23	May 15	May 28	May 19	May 11
Pentecost	May 30	May 22	June 4	May 26	May 18

	1998 C	1999 A	2000 B	2001 C
Ash Wed.	Feb. 25	Feb. 17	Mar. 8	Feb. 28
Lent 1	Mar. 1	Feb. 21	Mar. 12	Mar. 4
Lent 2	Mar. 8	Feb. 28	Mar. 19	Mar. 11
Lent 3	Mar. 15	Mar. 7	Mar. 26	Mar. 18
Lent 4	Mar. 22	Mar. 14	Apr. 2	Mar. 25
Lent 5	Mar. 29	Mar. 21	Apr. 9	Apr. 1
Passion Sunday	Apr. 5	Mar. 28	Apr. 16	Apr. 8
Holy Thur.	Apr. 9	Apr. 1	Apr. 20	Apr. 12
Good Fri.	Apr. 10	Apr. 2	Apr. 21	Apr. 13
Easter Day	Apr. 12	Apr. 4	Apr. 23	Apr. 15
Easter 2	Apr. 19	Apr. 11	Apr. 30	Apr. 22
Easter 3	Apr. 26	Apr. 18	May 7	Apr. 29
Easter 4	May 3	Apr. 25	May 14	May 6
Easter 5	May 10	May 2	May 21	May 13
Easter 6	May 17	May 9	May 28	May 20
Ascension Day	May 21	May 13	June 1	May 24
Easter 7	May 24	May 16	June 4	May 27
Pentecost	May 31	May 23	June 11	June 3